Practising Theory

Practising Theory

A guide to becoming an effective
adult education programmer

Anne Percival

University Extension Press

Extension Division
University of Saskatchewan

Printed in Canada
10 9 8 7 6 5 4 3 2 1   02 01 00 99 98 97 96 95 94 93

The following publishers have generously given permission to use extended quotations from copyrighted works:

Excerpts from articles in the *Canadian Journal of University Countinuing Education* reprinted with the permission of the Editor.

Excerpts from "Instructional Design for Distance Learning," by Jocelyn Calvert, in *Instructional Design: New Alternatives for Effective Education and Training*, by Kerry A. Johnson and Lin J. Foa, used by permission of American Council on Education and The Oryx Press, 4041 N. Central at Indian School Rd., Phoenix, AZ 85012, (602) 265–2651.

Excerpts from *The Organization and Planning of Adult Education* by T. J. Kowalski reprinted by permission of the State University of New York Press. Copyright © 1988 by T. J. Kowalski.

Excerpts from *Ethical Issues in Adult Education* by Ralph Brockett, ed. (New York: Teachers College Press, © 1988 by Teachers College, Columbia University; all rights reserved.) reprinted by permission of the publisher.

Excerpts from *Principles of Instructional Design* (3rd ed.) by R. M. Gagne, copyright © 1988 by Holt, Rinehart and Winston, Inc., reprinted by permission of the publisher.

Excerpts from "Training Adult Educators in North America" by S. B. Merriam and "Philosophical Orientations of Adult Educators" by L. McKenzie, in *Training Educators of Adults: The Theory and Practice of Graduate Adult Education*, edited by S. D. Brookfield, reprinted by permission of Routledge, Ltd.

Excerpt from p. 64 of *Developing Programs in Adult Education* by E. J. Boon, 1985, reprinted by permission of Prentice-Hall, Inc., Englewood Cliffs, NJ.

Canadian Cataloguing in Publication Data
Percival, Anne

Practising theory: a guide to becoming an
effective adult education programmer
ISBN 0–88880–288–9

1. Adult education – Canada.   I. University of
Saskatchewan. Extension Division.   II. Title.

LC5215.P47 1993   374   C93–098125–1

Contents

CONTENTS

Chapter III

Continuing Education: The Practice of Adult Education in Universities • 29

Chapter IV

Adult Learners • 53

Chapter V

Continuing Education Practice • 73

Chapter VI

Elements in Program Development • 89

Chapter VII

Professional Development in Continuing Education • 139

Appendix • 155

Foreword

About This Manual

This manual owes its existence to adult educators in university continuing education units across Canada. The majority of these individuals found themselves with the title "adult educator" before they fully understood what the term meant. Most were hired without any formal training in adult education and without experience in university continuing education. They learned about the requirements of their jobs, and about the meaning of adult education, on-the-job and through their own professional development efforts.

These pages contain, often in their own words, what these adult educators feel it is necessary to know, and the skills one has to have, to become an effective adult educator within the context of the university. Be cautioned, however—this manual is a guide for continuing education practice; it is not a "how to" manual. You will learn about your practice through your day-to-day experiences in continuing education. And you will grow as an adult educator by critically reflecting on your experiences and by actively pursuing opportunities for professional development.

Although this book was written specifically for those who work in university continuing education units, you will discover that much of the material applies to technical institutes and community colleges as well.

If someone would have said to me [when I first started in continuing education], "Here, read this book on adult education first," that would have really helped me. I was concentrating on what to say to students and the mechanics of the job, but it would have been a good idea if someone had said, "Read this book over the next three months and think about these things as they apply to your position." It would have helped me to get some background first and then learn the administrative things. You know, you just learn the administrative things as you go along (Rene).

The introductory chapter outlines the purposes of the manual and the assumptions that shaped its development. It provides ideas about how to use the manual and what to do during your early days on the job.

Chapter II provides an overview of the field of adult education by looking at what adult education is and why we do it. It emphasizes the importance of developing a rationale for practice and explains how to go about doing this. This chapter also introduces Canada's impressive tradition in adult education, as well as adult education practice in international settings.

Chapter III focuses on the practice of adult education in university settings and the importance of understanding the university context. It looks at university continuing education practices across the country so that you can get some sense of how your unit "fits in."

Chapter IV is concerned with adult learners—who they are, why they participate, and how they learn. Its purpose is to help you understand how to facilitate meaningful adult learning.

Chapter V looks at continuing education practice. It provides an overview of the professional functions of adult educators and focuses in on the program development function.

Chapter VI discusses each component of program development, from needs assessment to evaluation, in greater detail.

Chapter VII emphasizes the importance of professional development and provides sources for information and ideas about how to go about developing a personal professional development plan.

A bibliography listing the citation for every reference used in the manual is the last major section, followed by an index that will help you locate information of interest.

Regarding the format, quotations from interviews with continuing educators and from adult education literature are placed on the side panels of many of the pages in the manual. They reinforce the material in the text and, at the same time, provide you with opportunities to stop and reflect.

The quotations from interviews with continuing educators are in italics. Their contributions deserve special attention because they give you a sense of the complexity of continuing education practice that is often missing from adult education literature. They represent many points of view, and their voices ring with wisdom and experience. Pseudonyms are used to ensure anonymity.

Acknowledgements

This manual was first conceived ten years ago. At the time, I was a struggling neophyte in continuing education, knee-deep in trial-and-error learning. I remember thinking that someone should write an orientation manual for continuing educators because there had to be an easier way to discover some of the things that I needed to know to become an effective practitioner.

I am indebted to Dr. Stephen D. Brookfield, my dissertation advisor in the Adult Education Guided Independent Study (AEGIS) Doctoral Program at Teachers College, Columbia University, who recognized the value of this project and who provided ongoing support and encouragement as the work progressed. I am also grateful to the many continuing educators across Canada who participated in the project; their sincere interest in this undertaking and their willingness to devote time and energy to its completion provided the affirmation that I needed. Over seventy continuing educators, representing twelve universities, completed an initial needs-assessment questionnaire. Twenty of these individuals participated in follow-up interviews. The first draft of the orientation manual was evaluated by ten individuals who had participated in the interviews, ten continuing educators who had not, and a jury of continuing education "experts" identified by the 1991–92 Canadian Association for University Continuing Education (CAUCE) Executive.

As tends to be the case with such endeavours, the most important support for this project came from family members—my husband, Adrian, and my son, John. This manual is dedicated to these two special people.

Chapter I

Introduction

As children, may of us grew up dreaming about becoming astronauts or doctors; few of us grew up wanting to become adult educators.

Most of us come to this field via assorted and roundabout routes—through the "back door," as some describe it. We bring knowledge and experiences that are meaningful to our work, but often they are more directly related to the content of adult education programming or to a specialized program development skill than to the field of adult education. For example, we may be recruited because we have experience training in industrial settings or expertise in instructional design, small business consulting, language training, nursing, or other academic disciplines and professions.

Ironically, most of us begin our careers as adult educators knowing little about adult education, about how adults learn, or about continuing education practice. If we have never worked in a university, we have little knowledge about the culture and the practices of this kind of organization. Yet when you ask adult educators in university settings what one needs to know to be effective in this context, all of this knowledge is identified as being important. From the moment that we begin our careers,

orient ('ɔəriɛnt, ɔəri'ɛnt) *v* . . . 2. *fig. To adjust, correct, or bring into defined relations, to known facts or principles; refl. to put oneself in the right position or relation; to ascertain one's "bearings," find out "where one is." Also, to assign or give a specific direction or tendency to (The Compact Oxford English Dictionary, 1991, p. 1,225).*

1

We don't have a formal orientation program. Typically what we do is prepare a reading file for a new person coming on stream and each staff person spends some time with the new person. . . . We want [to recruit] people who have content expertise plus adult education background and awareness but that is a very difficult combination to come up with. . . . New people tend to have experience in the content area but very little adult education background, and we have to try to integrate them into the philosophy of adult education and give them the background (Ronnie).

When I first started [in continuing education], there was a lot of stress and tension on my part, thinking, "Am I doing this right? Am I going to be able to handle all of this?" When you are coming into an environment that is completely different and you are expected to understand that environment in order to do the work, there is bound to be stress. Having something like a manual that gave me some background and a framework would have made things a lot easier (Sandy).

then, we are apprenticing as adult educators. We learn in a variety of ways: on-the-job, from experienced colleagues, through reading and self-study, through participation in professional associations, and eventually, for some, through academic study.

This orientation manual is intended to start you off, give you your bearings, and point you in the right direction—in the direction of becoming an adult educator. It will, I hope, serve as a reference and a guide that will help to ease the initial stages of your transformation.

Becoming an adult educator is not a simple matter. As one continuing educator interviewed for this manual put it, "I have to know a lot about a lot of things." You also have to learn to apply your knowledge in different settings and with different people. The last chapter of this manual, which deals with professional development, suggests that there is an artistry to professional practice. Artistry is not something that you can learn from manuals or textbooks, but neither is it likely to be learned from experience alone. Artistry depends on a balance and an interaction between theory and practice, and it requires, in the words of another continuing educator, that you adopt a "THINK-DO" approach to practice. The development of this manual was guided by the belief that effective practice requires that you develop a rationale for what you do, a rationale that is based on principles of adult education and that is informed by your experiences as an adult educator. It takes time and a commitment to professional development to become an adult educator.

One of the difficult things about joining a university continuing education division is figuring out what you need to know and knowing what to ask. Since each university has its own practices and each program its own characteristics, this manual cannot tell you everything you need to know. What it attempts to do is:

- alert you to the kinds of knowledge and the skills that are required for practice

- help you identify issues that are of concern to adult educators

- stimulate your thinking and help you ask questions about continuing education practice within your own university

- get you thinking about your own assumptions and beliefs about adult learning

- give you ideas about how you can go about furthering your own development as an adult educator.

There are some important things that you should understand about this manual before you read further.

1. Although sections of the manual will be useful for teachers and counsellors of adults and for those responsible for the administration of the continuing education unit, the manual is intended for those who are involved in *program development* (i.e., in the design and management of adult education programs). The majority of adult educators who work full time in university continuing education perform program development functions.

2. The manual is written specifically for new continuing educators who have no prior training in adult education and/or no experience in university continuing education. If you are entering the field with prior training or related programming experience, sections of the manual will be familiar to you.

3. The manual attempts to provide you with an overview of the field and, as one continuing educator put it, the "mountain tops" of practice, but it is not comprehensive. Some topics are not dealt with, and many are not discussed in detail. Instead, the manual is intended to give you a "big picture" look at the field and the many components of practice.

4. The manual is concerned with how you develop meaningful educational experiences for adults, as opposed to the subject matter knowledge required to develop such experiences. Subject matter knowledge may be relevant to your work, but the assumption is that you either have, or have access to, this knowledge. For example, if your responsibilities include developing continuing education for nurses, the manual will not tell you anything about nursing or the requirements of professional education.

5. The manual is not a "how-to" guide for continuing education practice. As you will soon discover, each practice

If someone comes [into continuing education] with no experience in the field, they have to be open to their own continuing education. This almost needs to be negotiated in the hiring process and organized almost that first week [on the job]. Let's figure out what knowledge you need to acquire, what kinds of skills you need, and how you are going to get them (Terry).

There is a lot of decision making involved in [continuing education practice], and you get better at it over time, as you go along. You become more aware. . . . [New continuing educators] shouldn't have unrealistic expectations of themselves. They shouldn't expect to perform at the same level as someone with experience. They should expect to perform like someone who is new (Gerry).

My first year was pretty difficult. We didn't have the infrastructure we have right now and we didn't have the dean we have now. I didn't receive any guidance, to be very honest, during that first year. . . . It was very difficult for me because I didn't know what to ask. I didn't know what was involved. I had a certain amount of information that allowed me to keep things going, but it was very much by the seat of my pants (Morgan).

situation is unique and must be understood and acted upon accordingly. The manual provides some general guidelines for what you might do, but the point is made throughout that what you will do will depend upon your assessment of the factors that characterize your situation.

How to Use the Manual

Getting Around in the Manual

All authors hope that their work will be read from cover to cover. I confess to such hopes, but as someone who works in continuing education, I know that time is precious. The manual has been designed to be read from start to finish, or if time or your personal style favours, you can start with any chapter or any section. As much as possible, each section of the manual has been designed as a stand-alone module so that you can use a "grazing" or, as someone described it, a "smorgasbord" approach to your reading. Where a section introduces material covered in another chapter, the chapter is cross-referenced for your convenience. There is also an index to help you find subject and author references.

When You Need More Information

For each section of the manual, there is a list of suggested readings so that you can pursue ideas (and authors) of interest. Many of the suggested readings are recognized "standards" in the field of adult education. A conscious effort was made to include readings that can be found in most university education libraries (or on your colleagues' shelves). Use the bibliographies from these sources to expand your study of a topic. Chapter VII also lists some "classics" in the field as well as several key adult education journals. Finally, the Bibliography gives details of publication for each reference cited in the manual.

Relating What You Read to the Practices of Your Continuing Education Unit and Your University

Each chapter will help you to identify issues around, and questions about, practices and procedures in your own setting. Many sections in the manual end with a few "Questions to Ask," but reading the material should trigger other questions for you. Use these questions and the section themes to initiate discussions with your supervisor or some of your colleagues around what is done and why.

Identify somebody that you can use as a role model. It is pretty important because that is how you are going to learn. Or it's trial and error, which is a hard way to learn sometimes (Terry).

Getting Started in Continuing Education

If you are reading this manual, I hope that it was given to you as part of an orientation program developed by your continuing education unit. If this is not the case, some of the suggestions that follow may be useful to you.

1. If no one has been assigned to work with you directly, find out who you are to go to with your questions.

2. Ask for copies of calendars and promotion materials put out by your unit. Review these to get a sense of who does what internally.

3. Ask for an organizational chart.

4. Find out if there is a mission statement or an annual report for your unit. Are there planning documents available for the unit or the individual program areas?

5. Get to know your colleagues in the unit. Find out who does what. Who are the directors and supervisors of program and support areas and what are their responsibilities? What are the responsibilities of colleagues in your area, and in other program areas? Ask if you can meet with them to find out more about what they do.

Find out where your resources are. Find out who to ask and who is going to help you. Secretaries often know more about how programs run than anybody, so go to them. . . . Ask for advice, but don't ask them to do the job for you (Blair).

Another piece of advice for a new person coming into continuing education would be, "Trust yourself, trust your instincts, even though this is a new way of using your expertise" (Ronnie).

6. To begin to understand the internal administrative system, ask for copies of:

- policy and procedure documents. These may be at the level of the university (e.g., academic policies, collective agreements, policies of support services), the continuing education unit (e.g., record-keeping policies, approval processes for programs, GST guidelines, appeals procedures, by-laws of faculty or department council, promotion and tenure procedures, copies of terms of reference for standing committees, procedures for desktop publishing), or the program area (e.g., guidelines for instructors, copies of terms of reference for advisory committees, registration and refund policies, policies regarding exemptions, or transfers of credit).

- forms that you will fill out (e.g., expense forms, budget and purchase order forms, requisition forms for equipment, room reservation forms).

- copies of standard letters (e.g., instructor appointments, grades, graduation, grade appeals, letters of attendance). If there are no form letters, ask if you can have copies of existing letters to use as examples.

- a telephone book for your university.

7. Ask questions and use your colleagues as your most important resource.

Chapter II

Overview of the Field of Adult Education

What Is Adult Education?
(and a few related terms)

"Ah!" I hear you say, "we are going to start with something simple: a definition." In fact, there is probably no better way to get a sense of the complexity and scope of adult education than by looking at ways in which the term has been used.

What is generally agreed upon is that there is a distinction between the education of adults and adult education. The *education of adults,* a broad and inclusive term, encompasses all organized and purposeful attempts by adults to learn or to be assisted in learning. The term *adult education* is more restrictive and refers to activities that have been designed especially for adults (Selman and Dampier, 1991).

Consider the comments by the continuing educator on the side panel of the following page. First, Lee recommends that you take an overview course in some dimension of adult education. Presumably, such a course would be designed especially for adults and would fall into the definition of adult education. But what about Lee's second recommendation, that

This section is a "must read" if you think that adult education is simply the education of adults.

[One] piece of advice that I would suggest to new staff . . . is that they begin to develop a broader sense of what the field is about. That includes to, pretty quickly, get a course or two under their belts. . . . It doesn't have to be a course, it could be reading that is self-directed. Read some of the materials. There are some excellent texts out on adult education, adult learning, facilitating adult education. [New continuing educators need to] get some sense of where what they are doing fits into the broader context of adult and continuing education (Lee).

you undertake a self-directed or independent learning project? Whether or not this activity falls within the definition of adult education is less clear. Some say yes, arguing that the element of design is more crucial than the presence, or absence, of a teacher (Darkenwald and Merriam, 1982); others say no, arguing that an "educational agent" is a critical component of the definition of adult education (Verner and Booth, 1964, p. 1).

However this issue is decided, Knowles (1977) has pointed out that the definition of adult education that includes all of those organized, purposeful activities engaged in by adult learners in our society is only one usage of the term.

- Adult education has also been used to describe an academic discipline; that is, the study of how adults learn and how they can be assisted to learn.

- Adult education frequently is used to refer to a field of endeavour (see the title of this chapter); essentially, the field includes everyone who is involved with and concerned about the education of adults, regardless of where we work or what we do.

If adult education seems a bit too nebulous for you, consider the following definitions. The first is a definition that was developed by UNESCO and approved by member states in 1976. It recognizes adult education that occurs within the traditional or formal system of education, but it also acknowledges the vast amount of organized, nonformal adult education that happens within grass-roots movements, social movements, and a range of voluntary associations and community groups. Self-directed learning can also be included within this definition. According to Selman and Dampier (1991, p. 4), this "somewhat cumbersome, but inclusive definition" of adult education is probably the one that is most commonly cited.

> . . . the entire body of organized educational processes, whatever the content, level and method, whether formal or otherwise, whether they prolong or replace initial education in schools, colleges and universities as well as in apprenticeship, whereby persons regarded as adult by the society to which they belong develop their abilities, enrich their knowledge, improve their technical or professional qualifications or turn them in a new direction and bring

about changes in their attitudes or behaviour in the two-fold perspective of full personal development and participation in balanced and independent social, economic and cultural development. . . . (UNESCO, 1980, p. 3).

The second definition is one that Courtney (1989) offers to adult education practitioners. It is simple and open-ended, recognizing that to say more about the nature of adult education activities requires knowledge about the context in which the practitioner works and the purposes behind the practitioner's activities.

Adult Education is an intervention into the ordinary business of life—an intervention whose immediate goal is change, in knowledge or in competence. An adult educator is one, essentially, who is skilled at making such interventions (p. 24).

This manual includes all of the ways that Knowles says the term adult education has been used; however, generally it is used to refer to the educational activities, or to use Courtney's term, the "interventions," that continuing educators in university settings are involved in planning and administering. Essentially, this manual is concerned with what we do, why we do it, and how we do it.

We have considered two very different attempts to define adult education. But what about some other terms that you may have heard, terms like *continuing education* or *extension education*? These terms have particular relevance to universities and are reflected in the titles that universities use to describe their adult education units.

Continuing education means the same thing as adult education to most adult educators; however, the connotation that the adult learner is "building on," or continuing, his or her education has led to this term being favoured by secondary and post-secondary institutions (e.g., The University of Manitoba's Continuing Education Division and the University of Toronto's School of Continuing Studies).

Extension education is another phrase that has come to be associated with the adult education activities of universities (e.g., The University of Regina's University Extension and the

"Adult education is defined as all organized educational activities—everything from job-related training to hobby classes—taken outside of a full-time program. However, those who were engaged in self-education projects are not included as participants" (Devereaux, 1984, p. 1).

Note: This definition was used in a 1983 national study of participation in adult education that determined that one in every five Canadians seventeen years of age and over participated in at least one adult education activity.

"Terminology abounds: adult education, continuing education, lifelong learning, independent learning projects, community education, community development, adult learning, andragogy, adult basic education, animation, facilitation, conscientization. These terms have all been used at one time or another to mean more or less the same thing. As some have noted with particular frustration, 'the field of adult education has evolved a vocabulary possibly unparalleled in its confusion' " (Peterson, quoted in Courtney, 1989, p. 15).

University of New Brunswick's Department of Extension and Summer Session). The term originated in Britain and the connotation is one of extending the traditional knowledge and resources of the university to those who are not part of the traditional university audience. The term is also connected with agricultural education in rural settings and with some of the earliest adult education activities conducted in Canada.

For the purposes of this manual, the term continuing education is used to describe adult education within the context of the university. The term continuing education unit (CEU)[1] is used to describe the administrative unit within the university that is responsible for continuing education. A continuing educator (CE) is someone who works in a CEU and who is involved in some way in developing and administering adult education programs.

This discussion does not do justice to the wealth of terms that are used in relation to adult education. If you would like more information on the ways that adult education is conceptualized, the suggested readings at the end of this section may interest you.

Before you leave this section, consider the following questions.

1. What is the difference between adult education and adult learning? As Darkenwald and Merriam state, "All education surely involves learning, but not all learning involves education" (1982, p. 6).

2. For the purposes of adult education, how should we define adult? Are we referring to one's chronological years, social roles and responsibilities, or perhaps something else? Notice how the UNESCO definition of adult education deals with this issue.

3. If you agree with the idea that adult education includes those educational activities that we, as adults, often undertake on our own, how would you classify a TV documentary on the environment or a play like Henrik Ibsen's *A Doll's House*?

---

[1] Elsewhere, CEU is often used to refer to "Continuing Education Unit," a measure of both formal and nonformal learning that is widely used in the United States but that has much less application in Canada.

Again, consider the UNESCO definition of adult education. According to this definition, much of what is legitimately adult education occurs outside the formal system of education and is organized by people who, in all likelihood, do not identify themselves as adult educators.

Suggested Readings

Courtney, S. "Defining Adult and Continuing Education." In *Handbook of Adult and Continuing Education*, edited by S. B. Merriam and P. M. Cunningham, 15–25. San Francisco: Jossey-Bass, 1989.

Darkenwald, G. G., and S. B. Merriam. *Adult Education: Foundations of Practice*. New York: Harper & Row, 1982.

Selman, G., and P. Dampier. *The Foundations of Adult Education in Canada*. Toronto: Thompson, 1991.

Why Do We Do Adult Education? Purposes and Philosophies

This section introduces the importance of having a sound adult education philosophy to guide practice. It begins with a brief introduction to what theorists and continuing educators say about philosophy, considers a philosophical debate that is current within the practice of adult education in North America, and, finally, looks at how continuing educators can develop their personal philosophy of adult education.

This section is a "must read" if you believe that your purpose as a continuing educator is to achieve high enrolments and profitability.

Philosophy and Adult Education

We start with the assumption that there are no givens in conducting adult education. Why we do adult education, and how we go about doing it, are not based on any neutral prescriptions for practice. Our purposes are based on our values and beliefs about what adults should be like and how they ought to

I think one needs to help [new continuing educators] to articulate their own mission. I think that would be very useful. You know, questions related to "why am I here?" (Morgan)

behave. Values and beliefs, in turn, are expressions of philosophical assumptions, or theories, about "how things really are" or how things "should be." In other words, whether or not we choose to think about philosophy, we define our purposes and we act on the basis of philosophical assumptions (Blakely, 1957).

In a formal sense, "philosophy is interested in the general principles of any phenomenon, object, process, or subject matter. . . . Principles are the foundations or basic structures by which phenomena, events, and realities are understood" (Elias and Merriam, 1980, p. 3). Philosophy addresses such ponderous issues as what is reality, what is the nature of being human, what is the nature of society—and the answers arrived at have implications for the purposes, content, and instructional methods used in adult education.

A philosophy of adult education, then, is the *theory*[2] behind what you do as an adult educator. It serves as the guiding principle for your practice by giving direction and purpose to your day-to-day decision making. Another perhaps less intimidating way to think about this is that your practice as an adult educator requires that you have a sound adult education rationale on which to base your decisions.

If decision making is not based on a well-reasoned, defensible personal philosophy of adult education, then on what basis does someone involved in continuing education make decisions?

- There is a danger that decisions will be based on "hidden and uncritically assimilated assumptions" (Brookfield, 1987, p. 8) about adults and adult education that, if exposed, would not stand up to scrutiny.

I have to re-emphasize the necessity for people to really know where they are coming from in terms of their values and beliefs (Pat).

- An individual may let others do the thinking, essentially providing reasons and direction for action. The problem here is that the decisions taken may have nothing to do with a philosophy of adult education. They may reflect

---

[2] A theory is simply an explanation of our observations about some phenomenon and about how these observations relate to each other. If we understand how behaviours are related, we can act in ways to try to achieve certain outcomes. In this way, theories provide guidelines or principles for our actions.

organizational needs for high enrolments or profitability, or the agendas of other individuals and groups involved in the program, like heads of academic departments or advisory groups.

So, you ask, what is *the* philosophy of adult education? Having witnessed some of the difficulties surrounding definitions of adult education, it will probably come as no surprise that, indeed, there are several different philosophical traditions that are relevant to adult education. Each philosophical tradition is represented by the writings of several theorists, and each has different implications for the practice of adult education.[3]

Elias and Merriam (1980) use the following framework in their discussion of philosophical traditions:

- humanism

- behaviourism

- liberalism

- progressive education

- radical education

- analytic philosophy.

Hiemstra (1988) discusses the first five philosophical traditions that are included in the Elias and Merriam framework and adds two more: idealism and realism.

An adequate review of these philosophies and their implications for the practice of adult education is beyond the scope of this manual; however, a summary of each philosophy, along with the names of representative theorists, is included in the Appendix. The next section, which relates what continuing educators say about practice to major philosophical traditions, will also provide you with insight into the relationship between philosophy, or theory, and practice.

[New continuing educators] have got to have some notion in their minds about what they are trying to do here. What does it mean to provide programs, and who are these adults you are talking about? Why is what you do different from everything else? What is important about it? And I think that those are some of the things that they have got to come to terms with themselves (Gerry).

The thing about philosophy is it's often in the back of your head— it's not necessarily verbalized—but you live it (Blair).

---

[3] Chapter IV looks at some of the theories of learning that have developed from the philosophical traditions discussed in this section.

"... All practitioners make decisions and act in ways that presuppose certain values and beliefs. Whether or not it is articulated, a philosophical orientation underlies most individual and institutional practices in adult education. An evaluation of one's own philosophical orientation is one factor that distinguishes a professional adult educator from a nonprofessional or a novice" (Darkenwald and Merriam, 1982, p. 37).

How Continuing Educators Talk About Philosophy

The following statements were taken from interviews with continuing educators. They were made in response to questions about what continuing educators think is important and satisfying about their work. Although no one was asked to talk about adult education philosophy, these quotes clearly hint at different philosophical assumptions.

In reading these statements, two points should be kept in mind:

1. These statements are used to illustrate general philosophical traditions; however, within each tradition, one can find different points of view.

2. These statements, although perhaps typical, do not exhaust the range of philosophical orientations. What they do illustrate is that, even within the context of continuing education, there is no consensus about what the purposes, content, and methodology of adult education should be.

Radical Adult Education: An Example

"I think a lot of people want to know [that] what they are doing makes some difference in people's lives. And I have a struggle with that because, I argue with myself all the time, what I am really doing is supporting the existing status quo. People who already have are getting more. I'm really creating a gap between those who have and those who have not" (Gerry).

Just over the past year, I have come to realize that the things that I value are not the things that [my advisory committee] values. . . . I feel that there are times when I have really been at odds with them (Les).

According to this tradition, all education is value-laden. Like Paulo Freire (1970), a Brazilian educator who advocates radical social change through adult education, this continuing educator sees all education as political activity. It either liberates the disadvantaged or it supports a status quo that oppresses them. In this view, the purpose of education should be social change. The role of the teacher, who is also a learner, is to engage adults in dialogue about the cultural circumstances of their lives. Through problem-posing and dialogue, adults become conscious of the forces that control their lives, and empowered with this knowledge, they can act to bring about change.

Liberalism: An Example

"But if I can give [ideas] some shape and body so that they can become much more accessible to people who normally are not prone to seeing that the world of thought can be relevant to them, that is the greatest joy that I derive" (Robin).

Liberalism, which is the oldest philosophical tradition, derives from the writings of classical Greek philosophers. According to this tradition, humans have the ability to reason and freedom comes from developing this capacity. Cultivation of the intellect, then, is the purpose of adult education. The curriculum is focused on liberal studies, and the teacher, whose authority derives from the subject matter, assumes a traditional role. To some who support liberalism, a liberal education is essentially "morally, socially, and politically neutral" (Paterson, quoted in Darkenwald and Merriam, 1982, p. 44).

Behaviourism: An Example

". . . much of what we do is really needed, particularly in the business and the computer area. Most of the skills things that we do are really needed. And it is not a bad thing to go out and market things that are required and that are going to make a difference in people's lives. . . . It may seem like it is just a WordPerfect course or a Lotus course, but it could make the difference between keeping a job or losing a job. . . . I think that we have to be much more sensitive to what we are doing and what we are producing. . . . I would like to know that every time somebody goes to a business class, that the very next day when they go to work, they are able to apply things" (Stacey).

Behaviourism sees the goal of education as producing behaviour that fosters "survival" (e.g., job skills). According to this tradition, behaviour is the result of prior conditioning and is dependent on environmental forces. The role of the teacher is to arrange environmental contingencies such that the desired behaviour is produced and reinforced. Learning is defined as a change in overt behaviour and concern is with identifying measurable behavioural objectives. Adult education plays a role in helping individuals to adapt to technological and workforce changes, and in improving productivity and organi-

"... Many adult educators merely accept patterns of practice (and corresponding theoretical assumptions) to which they have been exposed without testing these patterns critically. . . . Adult education practice should include theoretical reflection. One of the differences between a proficient adult educator and a marginally effective adult educator is that the practice of the proficient adult educator refers continually to theoretical principles which allow the individual to move in a creative manner beyond repetitive actions. The marginally effective educator, confronted with totally novel situations, is unable to adapt to these situations on the basis of theoretical considerations" (McKenzie, 1988, p. 216).

... [Adult educators] need a strong commitment, some passion, to what they are doing and why they are doing it (Terry).

zational effectiveness. It is within this context—education and training for employees—that behaviourism has had its greatest impact on adult education.

Humanism: Some Examples[4]

"If we say that we are trying to meet the needs of students, if we say that our programs are learner-centred, how are we doing that? ... I try to do that by bringing learners on my [advisory] committee to get their perspectives" (Gerry).

"... to me, the most important thing that I do is any of those things that contribute, not to the smooth functioning of the program, but contribute to [students'] experiences or their success" (Les).

"I guess what I enjoy most is the sense of having made some kind of difference to individuals. My greatest satisfaction comes from ... assisting them along the way and then seeing them come back in a much more confident space, you know, having accomplished something for themselves, and feeling really good about themselves" (Ronnie).

Humanism sees the basic purpose of education as personal development or the self-actualization of the individual. Human beings have the capacity to make choices and, through their choices, to maximize their inherent potential. Since humanism views individuals as responsible for their own learning, education involves a learner-centred approach where learners participate in planning and evaluation and teachers act as facilitators. Since self-actualization is the goal, knowledge is highly personalized. Knowledge that is acquired through any learning experience is dependent on the needs, interests, and experiences of the individual. Malcolm Knowles (1980), in his presentation of andragogy—a model of assumptions about how adults learn—clearly has been influenced by the humanistic tradition. Chapter IV provides an overview of andragogy.

---

[4] Although humanism has had a tremendous impact on adult education in North America, the use of three quotes, as opposed to one to illustrate the other traditions, is not intended as a statement of the relative importance of humanism. The quotes suggest different aspects of humanism: learner involvement, learning through experience, and learner autonomy.

Do Adult Educators Agree on Any Philosophical Assumptions?

According to Beder (1989, p. 48), the following core principles are generally agreed upon by adult educators. These principles can be viewed as the foundation for all philosophies of adult education.

1. Whether society is basically good or inherently flawed, it can and should be improved. In this, adult education can and should play a major role.

2. If individuals, and ultimately society, are to prosper, learning must continue throughout life.

3. Adults are capable of learning and should be treated with dignity and respect.

4. All adults should have access to learning the things required for basic functioning in society.

5. Although adults may not differ from pre-adults in respect to the basic cognitive processes of learning, the context of adult education differs substantially from the context of pre-adulthood. Hence adults should be educated differently from pre-adults.[5]

Developing a Personal Philosophy of Adult Education

An adult education philosophy or rationale is a coherent set of assumptions about adult education and its relationship to individuals and to society. It gives purpose and direction to the decisions you make as an adult educator. In fact, given the number of decisions that are involved in developing or administering any program, having an understanding of why you do what you do is a requirement for ethical practice (Hiemstra, 1988).

The development of a personal philosophy of adult education begins with a critical examination of your own beliefs and assumptions about adult education and adult learning. You can

---

[5] For a discussion on facilitating adult learning, see Chapter IV.

begin this process by trying to answer questions like the following.

1. What is reality? What is knowledge?[6]

2. What is the difference between education and learning?

3. What does it mean to be human? Who is an adult?

4. What purposes should adult education serve? How does adult education relate to your ideas about human development or your vision of society?

5. What should the content of education be? What methods should be used?

6. How does your vision for adult education relate to the context in which you practice—that is, to continuing education and to your area of program responsibility?

Apps (1985) suggests that, in trying to answer questions such as these that go to the heart of personal beliefs, you are involved in a four-phase process.

1. Identifying the beliefs you hold about adults and about adult education.

2. Searching for contradictions among your beliefs.

3. Discovering the sources of your beliefs.

4. Making judgments about the beliefs you hold.

There are some other things that you need to keep in mind as you grapple with this issue of personal philosophy.

1. Identifying your beliefs is not an easy process. Do not be surprised if you cannot immediately come up with answers to questions like "what is reality?" (Apps, 1985).

2. Your thinking will be influenced by writers from different philosophical traditions and you may find it difficult to identify with any single tradition (Hiemstra, 1988). This is not unusual. In Chapter IV, principles for effective practice that are derived from humanism,

---

[6] Are these practical questions for new continuing educators? Your colleagues are not likely to ask you to describe what you mean by knowledge, but your assumptions about knowledge will influence your thinking—and the decisions you make—about adult education practice.

radical education, and progressive education are re-
viewed.

3. Your practice will influence your philosophy. Just as
reflection on assumptions helps you to formulate a
philosophy of adult education, reflection on practice
will lead you to accept, reject, or reformulate your
theory (Merriam, 1982).

Some of the following strategies may be helpful to you in
identifying your beliefs and in developing a personal philosophy.

1. Read what others say about philosophical issues. Be
careful not to uncritically adopt what others believe, or
what you think is "politically correct."

2. Attempt to write down your beliefs and assumptions.
This helps to expose weak links in your belief system.

3. Talk to your colleagues, experienced adult educators,
and learners about these issues. Again, this can be
useful in helping you to reflect on your beliefs.

4. Think about your own day-to-day experiences in practice. Try to be self-conscious about what you do; try not
to make decisions based on habitual ways of thinking
and acting.

5. Try to complete Hiemstra's (1988) "Personal Philosophy Worksheet," included in the Appendix. Hiemstra
gives his students the worksheet along with the suggestion that they follow one of three options, outlined by
Elias and Merriam (1980):

   i) pick a philosophy that best fits with your personal
   system of values and beliefs;

   ii) opt for an eclectic approach and choose elements
   from different philosophies; or

   iii) choose a philosophy as a framework but integrate
   elements from other philosophies that are not inconsistent with your basic position.

6. Complete Zinn's (1990) "Philosophy of Adult Education Inventory." The reference for the Inventory is
given in the suggested readings that follow this section.

"... Theory without practice leads to empty idealism, and action without philosophical reflection is mindless activism" (Darkenwald and Merriam, 1982, p. 37).

The Philosophical Debate in North America: Is Adult Education a Profession or a Movement for Social Change?

In Canada and the United States, a humanistic, individualistic orientation to adult education dominates practice. This orientation, combined with efforts to advance the professional status of adult education, has led adult education to become increasingly institutionalized and market driven (Selman and Dampier, 1991). It is a one-sided approach to adult education, and it has been criticized vehemently by adult educators who are committed to philosophical orientations that support adult education for social change, or who believe that job-oriented programming is displacing liberal adult education (Cunningham, 1989; Spencer and McIlroy, 1991). The tensions resulting from these philosophical conflicts are apparent in the adult education literature and also can be felt within some CEUs[7] (Cruikshank, 1991).

The issue of whether adult education should be viewed as an emerging profession, or as a broadly based movement for social change, has tended to polarize adult educators. On the one hand, there are those who argue for established standards of practice, professional training for adult educators, and research into adult learning (Houle, 1956). The majority of adult educators have accepted these general goals as appropriate for the field of adult education (Cameron, 1981). On the other hand, there are those who believe that attempts to professionalize adult education have had deleterious consequences for practice. They believe that professionalism has institutionalized adult education within the formally established system of schooling. This, in turn, has decreased the visibility of nonformal adult education and the likelihood that adult educators who work outside the formal system will be seen, or will identify themselves, as adult educators (Cunningham, 1989).

There is also the criticism that professionalism, combined with individualism, has turned some adult educators into mere technicians, experts in the "how to's" of needs assessment, program planning, marketing, and evaluation (Selman, 1985).

---

[7] The effects of philosophical conflicts within CEUs are discussed in Chapter III.

In giving learners responsibility for defining their needs, critics argue that adult educators have abdicated their responsibility to address broader social issues and problems (Mezirow, 1984a). According to this view, professionalism has encouraged a free-market, "felt needs," middle-class, job-related approach to education that has gone a long way toward displacing education for other purposes and for other people.

The debate has not been resolved to everyone's satisfaction; however, it has brought the philosophy of adult education to the foreground. There is little disagreement from anyone in the field, whether they support or question professionalism, that adult educators must be more than technicians or customer service representatives—first and foremost, they must be educators.

And this brings us back to the question that opened this discussion of philosophy: Why do we do what we do in adult education? Since adult educators cannot help but make value judgments in practice, they are responsible for ensuring that questions related to why they do what they do precede questions related to what and how. To do less must be regarded as unprofessional and unethical (Brockett, 1988).

A discussion about the "appropriate" purposes of continuing education is found in Chapter III.

Suggested Readings

Philosophy in Adult Education

Beder, H. "Purposes and Philosophies of Adult Education." In *Handbook of Adult and Continuing Education*, edited by S. B. Merriam and P. M. Cunningham, 37–50. San Francisco: Jossey-Bass, 1989.

Elais, J. L., and S. B. Merriam. *Philosophical Foundations of Adult Education*. Malabar, FL: Robert E. Krieger, 1980.

Merriam, S. B., ed. *Selected Writings on Philosophy and Adult Education*. Malabar, FL.: Robert E. Krieger, 1984.

Developing Your Own Philosophy

Apps, J. W. *Improving Practice in Continuing Education*. San Francisco: Jossey-Bass, 1985.

Hiemstra, R. "Translating Personal Values and Philosophy into Practical Action." In *Ethical Issues in Adult Education*, edited by R. G. Brockett, 178–94. New York: Teachers College Press, 1988.

Zinn, L. M. "Identifying Your Philosophical Orientation." In *Adult Learning Methods*, edited by M. W. Galbraith, 39–77. Malabar, FL: Robert E. Krieger, 1990.

THE PHILOSOPHICAL DEBATE

Cunningham, P. M. "The Adult Educator and Social Responsibility." In *Ethical Issues in Adult Education*, edited by R. G. Brockett, 133–45. New York: Teachers College Press, 1988.

Selman, G. "The Adult Educator: Change Agent or Program Technician." *Canadian Journal of University Continuing Education* 11 (October 1985): 77–86.

Read the books. Go to as many things as you can in the field. Join the [provincial] association. Become involved. This is how you are going to learn about the issues. This is how you are going to develop your own personal beliefs and values (Gerry).

Adult Education in Canada: Some Examples of Early Practice

This section is not intended as a history of the development of adult education in Canada. Historical accounts of some of the better-documented projects are listed under the suggested readings that follow. Instead, the purpose of this section is to introduce you, briefly, to two early examples of adult education practice in Canada: the Antigonish Movement and the National Farm Radio Forum. Projects like the Women's Institutes, Citizens' Forum, and Frontier College are also good illustrations of the work of early Canadian adult educators. These projects appeared prior to 1950, when adult education began to take on its institutional and market-driven characteristics (Selman and Dampier, 1991).

Historical accounts of the development of adult education practice in Canada are colourful and inspirational, but they seem far removed from the daily activities of present-day

This section is a "must read" if you think that, as with basketball and musical theatre, Canada lacks a significant tradition in adult education.

continuing educators. This is precisely why we need to read these accounts and to become familiar with the visions they portray. In describing roles for adult educators that few continuing educators have experienced, these projects remind us of the "communitarian" traditions that have characterized Canadian society and adult education practice in Canada. As Selman and Dampier put it, what distinguishes Canadians from Americans is "Canadians' greater confidence in government as an instrument of public benefaction, and the greater tendency in Canada to care for each other's welfare" (1991, p. 58).

Reading historical accounts of adult education practice in this country also forces us to ask questions about contemporary continuing education practice. Is an individualistic, market-driven focus for continuing education sufficient? Or, in the face of national and community concerns over issues like Canadian unity, economic recession and poverty, racism, the quality of public education, and protection of the environment, to name a few, do continuing educators not have broader social responsibilities?

The Antigonish Movement and Farm Forum are not included here because they are the best examples of early Canadian adult education practice, but because they are good examples. As it happens, both projects also had university involvement. In the case of Antigonish, St. Francis Xavier University was the backbone of the project; in the case of Farm Forum, universities played secondary, supportive roles. But, in both cases, universities worked with community groups and organizations to assist Canadians in meeting the challenges prescribed by the circumstances of their lives.

The Antigonish Movement and Farm Forum were projects rooted in efforts to promote social change by helping Canadians deal with problems created by factors like immigration, economic depression, and geography. Both projects earned international recognition, and both served as models for adult educators working in other countries. During the periods in which these projects flourished, adult education in Canada "could be said to have been a social movement, with goals of its own and with a vision of the kind of society it wished to create" (Selman and Dampier, 1991, p. 63).

"The Canadian adult education community is suffering from a severe case of historical amnesia. . . . If we do not grasp the continuities and discontinuities of past and present, we can easily become captive to oppressive ideologies and values of the present" (Welton, 1987a, p. 12).

More and more of the young people who are coming into our diploma programs in adult education have absolutely no idea at all about the Canadian tradition in adult education and I would argue very strongly that it is really important that [we have] a grounding in our own traditions (Pat).

Antigonish Movement

The "Antigonish Movement" was a co-operative education project begun in the 1920s by the Extension Department of St. Francis Xavier University in Antigonish, Nova Scotia. Under the direction of two priests, Father Moses Coady and Father James Tompkins, adult education programs, co-operatives, and a system of credit unions were established to assist impoverished farmers, fishermen, and unemployed industrial workers in this economically depressed region.

There was nothing very new or radical about the methods used by the Antigonish educators. They "believed that persons, awakened through education, would develop the strategies for co-operative economic institutions" (Lotz and Welton, 1987, p. 109). Through involvement in study clubs, people were encouraged to define their economic problems and, collectively, to work toward solutions. The title of Father Coady's book, *Masters of Their Own Destiny*, which was published in 1939, articulates clearly the philosophy of the Antigonish Movement.

The Extension Department at St. Francis Xavier University provided knowledge resources and trained leaders for the movement, but it suffered from the same financial problems that face contemporary universities. In 1938, at a time when the movement was at its peak and thousands of people were enroled in study clubs throughout the Maritimes, a report suggested that the University would have a difficult time continuing its financial support for the Extension Department. Fortunately, a federal grant was received that year and the financial crisis that constantly threatened the movement was averted (Lotz and Welton, 1987).

By 1939, this grass-roots co-operative movement had resulted in the establishment of 342 credit unions and 162 other co-operative organizations, including lobster factories and sawmills, throughout the Maritimes. Coady died in 1959, and the movement effectively died with him (Lovett, Clarke, and Kilmurray, 1983).

Antigonish stands as Canada's best known—and some would argue best—example of adult education for community development and social reform.

National Farm Radio Forum

National Farm Radio Forum was a joint effort of the Canadian Broadcasting Corporation (CBC), the Canadian Association for Adult Education (CAAE), and the Canadian Federation of Agriculture (CFA). E. A. Corbett, the first director of CAAE, was responsible for initiating this project, as well as a similar project known as Citizens' Forum (Faris, 1975).

Broadcast from 1941 to 1965, National Farm Radio Forum involved rural Canadians from across the country in discussions of a wide range of topics. The project used print material, broadcasts, discussion groups, and feedback on the reactions of discussion groups to promote a sense of national community and to assist community groups to deal with shared concerns. The Farm Forum motto—Read, Listen, Discuss, Act—reflected Corbett's belief that adult education activity should not only benefit individuals but that it should lead to collective community action (Brookfield, 1986).

A number of university extension units, recruited by CAAE, co-operated in Farm Forum by assisting with the production and mailing of discussion materials and by organizing local discussion groups.

Farm Forum was proposed as a model for mass education in developing countries by UNESCO, and, reportedly, over forty countries adopted the program in some form (Faris, 1975).

Citizens' Forum was a similar project initiated by Corbett in co-operation with the CBC. This project, which came on the heels of the Second World War, was another attempt by Corbett to use public affairs programming to help Canadians develop a sense of national identity (Selman and Dampier, 1991).

"Helping Canadians—all Canadians—to live a life and mold their world remains a major challenge for adult education and adult educators. To ignore this aspect of adult education's tasks in our society would run the danger of justifying the kind of charge which the leading Chartist newspaper hurled in its day, when it referred to educationists as 'the pretended friends, but the real enemies of the people' " (Selman, 1987, p. 48).

Suggested Readings

Cassidy, F., and R. Faris, eds. *Choosing our Future: Adult Education and Public Policy in Canada.* Toronto: OISE Press, 1987.

Faris, R. *The Passionate Educators.* Toronto: Peter Martin, 1975.

Kidd, J. R. *Adult Education in Canada.* Toronto: Canadian Association for Adult Education, 1950.

Lovett, T., C. Clarke, and A. Kilmurray. *Adult Education and Community Action: Adult Education and Popular Social Movements*. London: Croom Helm, 1983.

Selman, G., and P. Dampier. *The Foundations of Adult Education in Canada*. Toronto: Thompson, 1991.

Welton, M. R., ed. *Knowledge for the People: The Struggle for Adult Learning in English-Speaking Canada, 1828–1973*. Toronto: OISE Press, 1987.

Adult Education: A Global Activity

This section draws your attention to an obvious reality, but one that is sometimes overshadowed by our North American perspective. As a field of practice and as a discipline of study, adult education is an international activity. Just as our sense of what adult education is, and who adult educators are, is informed by history and by the traditions of Canadian practice, it is shaped by reading accounts that place adult education within a global context.

Before suggesting some sources for literature on international adult education, a few "global" generalizations about adult education as it is practised around the world are offered. Given how difficult it is to define and describe adult education within a North American context, generalizations about worldwide practice are of extremely limited value. However, they are offered here only to demonstrate the contextual nature of adult education practice and to illustrate that the philosophy that dominates North American practice is not shared by many adult educators in the global community.

In a review of world trends and issues in adult education, Bhola (1989) compares adult education philosophy and practice in free-market economies, centrally planned economies, and Third World or developing economies. Adult education in most free-market countries, especially since the Second World War, is characterized by a pragmatic individualism that, increasingly, emphasizes job-related training, productivity, and indi-

This section is a "must read" if you've never realized that, in addition to the literature on North American research and practice, a lot has been written about the study and practice of adult education around the world.

vidual self-reliance and problem solving.[8] Bhola notes that in recent years a "radical streak of activism that talks of organizing people to help themselves" (p. 27) has appeared in the West. Many new programs are focused on helping the disadvantaged, but, Bhola submits, these activities focus more on helping individuals adapt than on changing social structures. Other new, or renewed, interests in adult education can be found in worker education, education for the elderly, peace and disarmament education, and leisure education.

Centrally planned economies, according to Bhola, use adult education, both formally and nonformally, to promote political education as well as economic development. There are few good case studies of adult education in these economies; however, the importance given to adult education in the maintenance of political ideology has meant that literacy education has tended to be a central focus.

Developing countries, regardless of political ideology, see adult education as a strategy for, and as central to, the process of social, cultural, and economic development, in other words, to nation building (Bhola, 1989). The failure of 1960s modernization efforts, which relied heavily on technology transfer and capital investment, has led many adult educators to recognize that development requires changes to basic social structures and that people must be involved to effect structural changes. The radical views of theorists like Paulo Freire, who advocate consciousness-raising as a way to empower and mobilize people for change, have been adopted in many developing countries. Typically, adult education within this context is nonformal and includes community-based literacy programs, community development projects, and forms of popular education (Ewert, 1989).

For information on the study and practice of adult education in international settings, you can begin with the suggested readings at the end of this section, or you can refer to the following information sources.

1. *Convergence* and the *International Journal of Lifelong*

"To the extent that adult education practitioners and scholars are knowledgeable about adult education elsewhere and to the extent to which they themselves are engaged in a systematic, comparative analysis of their own and others' practice—both within and beyond their own national boundaries—to that same extent they are empowered to (1) continuously develop their overall adult education philosophy; (2) initiate meaningful reforms needed to confront fundamental issues surrounding the practice and study of adult education; and (3) introduce improvements in the ways they conceptualize the process of adult education" (Cookson, 1989, p. 80).

---

[8] For a discussion of the dominant North American approach to adult education, see Chapter II.

I think it would be useful for [new continuing educators] to get some source listings of materials that are not strictly within the somewhat narrow field of adult education as we define it, because I think that that is all changing, so I'm just arguing for stuff that is taken from the politics and the sociology of adult education. Most of this writing comes from the European context. . . . It's worth looking at some of the OECD documents that outline the goals of adult education, say, in developing countries (Pat).

Education are two journals that provide a forum for international adult education.

2. The Educational Resources Information Centre (ERIC), the major data base for adult education, contains references to a variety of international adult education publications, including those of UNESCO, the International Council for Adult Education (ICAE), and the Organization for Economic Co-operation and Development (OECD).

Suggested Readings

ISSUES AND CONCEPTS

Bhola, H. *World Trends and Issues in Adult Education*. London: Jessica Kingsley, 1989.

Coombs, P. *The World Crisis in Education: The View from the Eighties*. New York: Oxford University, 1985.

Ewert, D. M. "Adult Education and International Development." In *Handbook of Adult and Continuing Education*, edited by S. B. Merriam and P. M. Cunningham, 84–98. San Francisco: Jossey-Bass, 1989.

Jones, R. K. *Sociology of Adult Education*. Brookfield, VT: Gower, 1984.

MAJOR INFLUENCES ON INTERNATIONAL ADULT EDUCATION PRACTICE

Freire, P. *Pedagogy of the Oppressed*. New York: Herder & Herder, 1970.

Illich, I. *Deschooling Society*. New York: Harper & Row, 1970.

Chapter III

Continuing Education: The Practice of Adult Education in Universities

Understanding the University Context

If you have never worked in a university before, you may be in for a surprise. The university is a unique type of organization. This section introduces you to the university—its mission, organization, decision-making processes—and some of the implications that these characteristics have for continuing education practice.

The mission of the university can be captured in three words: teaching, research, and service. The following description of the university, offered by Dr. L. Harris, illustrates the teaching, research, and service functions as well as the university's strong liberal traditions that emphasize knowledge generation and the cultivation of the intellect. As Dr. Harris's description suggests, continuing education is one of the ways in which the university manifests its public service function.

> A university is a special kind of institution primarily concerned with higher education. Its status in society derives from several distinguishing characteristics.

This section is a "must read" if you think that, because you once attended university, it will be easy for you to adjust to working in this type of organization.

Many people coming in fresh to our kind of organization are incredibly confused about what our organization's culture is, what we stand for, how we relate to each other. . . . My experience has been that people coming in from a business environment will probably be shocked at how loose and uncoordinated we are in terms of our goals and our objectives, and I think that we don't see it that way (Pat).

In this institution, I would encourage anyone who comes in to put themselves, as much as possible, into the mainstream—to find out who the players are in the university and to really get involved (Ronnie).

. . . Overall, you could argue that, in the kind of setting that [continuing education] is in right now, [new continuing educators] need to be more politically astute. They need to understand universities and where [continuing education] fits into the whole field of campus politics. They need to be sensitized toward that (Pat).

- It is concerned with the encouragement and development of intellectual excellence.
- It seeks to foster the kind of education that makes for intelligent and sensitive citizenship and effective leadership.
- It provides a setting in which ideas of all sorts are developed, scrutinized, discussed and evaluated.
- It encourages its members to pursue knowledge both as a good in itself and as a means of solving some of the problems of a constantly and rapidly changing world.
- It makes its resources of learning available to the community at large.
- It trains adult students in the application of specialized knowledge.

To put it even more succinctly, the unique attributes of the university are demonstrated in liberal education, basic research, and professional training—its essential goals are the transmission to succeeding generations of the hard-won knowledge and wisdom of the past; the discovery of new knowledge and new wisdom that will elevate humanity's estate not merely in the material sense but in the way of liberated minds, cultivated imaginations and educated sensibilities; and the opening of windows and doors to the world of arts and letters, of science, of scholarship in its broad sense, of aesthetics, of philosophical speculation, of entrepreneurial temper, of dedication to truth and to the cultivation of such values as have led us from barbarism along the path to civilization (1988, p. 6–7).

Generally, the three components of the university's mission are not viewed by academics as being of equal importance. In particular, there is considerable ambivalence toward the role of public service (Campbell, 1984). A minority of academics view public service as inconsistent with the university's quest for knowledge, academic freedom, and integrity. At the other extreme, another group believes strongly that universities are obliged to provide service to the community. But, as Campbell points out, both these positions require a strong institutional commitment, and this is often missing in academics who iden-

30

tify, first and foremost, with particular disciplines of study. Too, even those who support public service rank it below research and teaching in overall importance to the university (Lynton and Elman, 1987).

The ambivalence surrounding the goals of universities can be understood in terms of other characteristics that set universities apart. The traditional line and staff positions that one finds in a corporate model of the organization are reversed in universities. Consequently, decision making is highly decentralized and variable. Clark (1983) notes that for policy decisions to have authority, they require support from those at all levels within the organization. The term "collegiality" is often used to describe this kind of decision making, where authority is given to the whole body. As Cyert (1985, p. 123) notes, each faculty member becomes in a sense a "private entrepreneur," generally an autonomous decision maker, but working through a system of democratically operated committees when required.

Universities also have been described as "loosely coupled" organizations that are closer to coalitions and federations than other organizational forms. Given the specialized interests of the academic community, loose coupling allows the component parts to evolve independently, to set their own goals, and to determine their own interests. These relationships make organizational change difficult, incremental, and uneven. While units like continuing education have the flexibility to develop new approaches and formats, loose coupling allows other units to entrench traditions that may appear archaic.

There is also a "bureaucratic ethos" within universities, particularly in the way that the administrative and support services of universities are managed (King and Lerner, 1987, p. 21). Admissions and registration, student records, and other business operations are governed by a bureaucratic culture that is focused on policies and procedures, and that is slow to adapt to pressures for change.

Campbell (1984) suggests that even when the rhetoric of universities is supportive of continuing education, as it often is, university policies reflect a different set of priorities. In particular, funding arrangements that have made continuing education largely—and increasingly—self-financing demonstrate the ambivalence that universities have toward their public-service

I dislike having to justify what we do and having to twist people's arms to get them to participate. I'm referring to other faculty members within the university—trying to convince them that distance education is a worthwhile thing to do. I don't like having to do that. I think I do a reasonably good job of getting the message through, but I seem to have to get it through to somebody new every time it comes out (Francis).

Just be aware of who does what and how the organization functions and who the movers and shakers are. . . . [A new continuing educator] really has to know, and each organization is totally different, how the organization ticks, functions, and where they should go and where they shouldn't go to get advice and assistance. And that takes time (Dale).

One of the things that I think people coming into this environment need, if they have never worked in a university before, is to learn to work in a collegial way. [Most people] are used to working in a fairly authoritarian structure, in a hierarchical structure, and there is much more collegiality here (Francis).

31

One example I have just kept track of—I have had almost forty meetings with one faculty member and deans and his chair on getting this person from the stage of thinking about doing a course to preparing the material, to signing a contract. . . . (Dale).

. . . It's the old pep talk for new staff about getting involved in division committees and getting involved in university committees (Lee).

Identify who you can work with out there and who can become your allies. . . . Know who your allies are because many decisions that affect you are made at department meetings and you are not going to be there. So develop [rapport] with individuals who can be your mentors or supporters (Dale).

I spend quite a bit of time on . . . relationships with academic colleagues on campus. And that is working not only on developing programs that pertain to their content area, but also interpreting what we are doing in the faculty [of continuing education] and in my department in particular (Pat).

responsibilities. The budget cutbacks experienced by many continuing education units in recent years have severely curtailed the ability of continuing education to provide certain types of programming.

Increasingly, CEUs are being forced to adopt the characteristics of an entrepreneurial model within the context of the university's academic model in order to survive. As an ideal type, the entrepreneurial model focuses on making money, on cost efficiency, and on operating like a small business (King and Lerner, 1987).

As the following chart illustrates, having public service as an important programming mandate creates differences and areas of potential conflict between continuing education and other academic units on campus.

Cultural Manifestations and Potential Conflicts[1]

The University	The Extension Division
• disciplinary program development	• cross-disciplinary program development based on learner needs
• serves faculty and established programs	• serves the community
• priority to full-time students	• serves the part-time student constituency
• power rests ultimately with faculty	• philosophically, power rests with learners, whose enrolment patterns determine many decisions
• conservative fiscal policies	• entrepreneurial fiscal policies
• discipline-oriented	• market-oriented
• rewards primarily to research output and quality	• rewards to program output and quality
• individual status from scholarly peers	• individual status from adult education and university peers
• purpose often no more specific than "teaching and research"	• purpose often specified by community need

[1] The illustrative characteristics listed here are those of an extension division embracing the philosophy of adult education (Blaney, 1986, p. 75. Used with permission of the *Canadian Journal of University Continuing Education*).

Functioning Within the University Context

To accomplish its programming mandate, a Continuing Education Unit must be able to mobilize the required resources of the university and to span the traditional boundaries between academic departments and disciplines.

Given the nature of universities as organizations, some implications of this for continuing educators are as follows.

1. Developing and maintaining good internal communication networks are not easy tasks, but they are essential for successful programming.

   The advice from both continuing educators and adult education theorists alike is to "get involved," in as many ways as you can, in the academic community and to cultivate those relationships that are important, or potentially important, to your programming activities (Apps, quoted in Cauthers, 1991). This will ensure that you have a voice in shaping policies that have consequences for continuing education's adult constituency.

2. Decision making within the university is variable, political, and time consuming. It depends on the values, interests, and influence of those involved. Knowing who the players are, understanding their viewpoints, and ensuring that you have an opportunity to explain the position of continuing education are important to developing good working relationships and to achieving the kinds of outcomes that will serve continuing education.

   Again, getting involved is the first step. Becoming sensitive to academic values and concerns is the second step. This entails being able to articulate a well-thought-out position in relation to these concerns—one that is based on educational arguments. As Blaney (1986, p. 76) suggests, within the university context "there is a shared belief in the power and the importance of learning." Diplomatic skills and good negotiating skills are definite assets for a continuing educator.

3. There is an attitude toward scholarship that is shared among members of the academy that sets the "academic" apart from the "entrepreneur."

I don't know that members of the institution really recognize what goes into . . . continuing education. It's up to us to tell them about that, but I think that we're so busy doing all these things that we don't always manage this dimension as well as we should (Jan).

Another important part is being able to guarantee to the academic department that the distance courses that I develop are going to meet their standards and follow their practices as much as possible. And, if they don't, I will have cleared that with the department and come to an agreement with them. . . . Universities are political and very territorial (Francis).

[I dislike] the politics of the organization, the time it takes to get things through. I just got approval about a week ago for a degree at a distance in psychology which has taken the better part of three years. The politics and the long time it takes to get acceptance of new ideas [is frustrating]. And you can't go forward. You can do a few things on the margin, but you still need to get mainstream acceptance of broad program objectives and long-term plans, otherwise [your proposal] is doomed to fail. . . . And [you have to] understand the politics and the players, and the players change and their priorities shift as well (Dale).

. . . With my own academic background, you worked on your own and you were not expected to collaborate with other people. In fact, that was looked down upon and discouraged. . . . (Morgan).

If you hire people with academic backgrounds, there may be a need to make people aware that [collaboration] is okay—that we are not in this for personal glory and this is not a competition. It's a matter of trying to do something collectively, and that's something that's admired and valued (Ronnie).

. . . I can't think that we do a very good job of orienting newcomers to the particular academic culture in which we work; basic issues such as interpersonal dynamics in dealing with colleagues—particularly the difficult, incompetent, eccentric, and creative ones—are often ignored (Pat).

Although some academics will continue to regard continuing education as a function that is inappropriate for the university, having competence in the philosophy of adult education[2] and its application within a university setting is the first step toward establishing yourself as a colleague and not as someone who simply "uses the university as a base for educational retailing" (Campbell, 1984, p. 106).

4. Academics tend to work independently. The idea of working collaboratively on an educational activity, like the design of materials for distance delivery, might seem foreign to them.

5. One inherent conflict that has been identified between the approach of most academics to education and the approach of continuing educators is that while many academics have a discipline or subject-centred approach to knowledge and concentrate on knowledge generation, continuing educators advocate a learner-centred, multidisciplinary approach that focuses on knowledge application (Lynton and Elman, 1987; Whale, 1987).

   Think about how this difference could affect definitions of "excellence" and "quality"; instructors who are members of the academy may have very different views than you, or than adult learners, about these terms. Again, having a sound adult education rationale or philosophy that is linked to the larger purposes of the university will help you to deal with these conflicts.

6. Most of your relationships with academic colleagues will be stimulating and rewarding, but be prepared for the occasional difficult relationship. Just as the university's structure allows for and accommodates widely disparate points of view, it can tolerate idiosyncratic temperaments and behaviours.

7. Not surprisingly, CEUs share some of the organizational characteristics of universities. In other words, CEUs tend to exhibit loose coupling and varied goals and interests related to programming—some of which can stem from

---

[2] See Chapter II for a discussion of the philosophies relevant to adult education.

different philosophical orientations and independent decision making.

Many continuing educators point with satisfaction to the independent nature of their work and the fact that they have freedom and flexibility to establish their own programming goals and to shape their activities. But if these characteristics are not well understood and addressed in some way by the CEU, the downside of this organizational arrangement can be poor internal communications, stronger identification with—and commitment to—one's programming goals than to the overall mission of the CEU, and competition over scarce resources.

In summary, what conclusions should you draw from this discussion? Probably very few. But be prepared. If you have worked in other organizations, you will find that the tempo is different within universities. Changes to policies or the introduction of new ideas can proceed slowly—lots of people may have something to say on such issues, and often committees that are responsible to larger bodies will be used to formulate recommendations regarding change. What may seem like minor opposition to a proposal can create a deadlock that becomes difficult to resolve. If you are very action-oriented—and many continuing educators are—expect a lot of talking. Things will get done, but instead of the rational model that you may be accustomed to, the decision-making process will seem more like "organized anarchy" (Cohen and March, 1974).

Expect, too, that some academics will be wildly enthusiastic about what you are doing, others will be much less supportive—a few may even be disdainful—and most will likely go on about their business without too much thought, one way or the other, about continuing education.

Since academic interests may be different from those of continuing education, you are wise to consider these interests when you formulate your proposals and when you interact with colleagues outside the CEU. Base your arguments on educational grounds, on your philosophy about adult education and its role within the university context. Be seen as an educator, not as a technician or a sales representative.

[New continuing educators] may see a microcosm in the extension area of what they perceive to be, to use the term that is most often used, the organized anarchy of the major campus situation. They can see that replicated in the continuing education unit . . . and they find it extremely discordant and confusing. I think that there is a logic to it and it's up to us to try and explain what that logic is (Pat).

This [CEU] needs to do some team/group building among staff. I can walk down the hall and I see somebody and they may or may not acknowledge me when I go by. They're a [program] coordinator. I'm a coordinator, but I've never been at a meeting where they have been. I don't know what they do—sometimes I don't even know their name. I can guess, and I've seen it on their door maybe. It's a real sense of isolation (Terry).

35

For a long time, there was a real fortress mentality among members of [the CEU] and real competition over the goodies. But over the last few years, that has changed a lot. There is a lot more crossing over among units as well as working better together in any given unit. . . . One of the things that has happened in our faculty is that instead of each area doing its own thing and not telling anybody outside of it what was going on, we have developed a number of . . . transfaculty positions. For example, the publications coordinator, the technological supervisor, . . . these people cross between the areas, work with all the areas, and pull people together to do things together (Francis).

Questions to Ask

1. Does your university have a mission statement that speaks to the importance of continuing education activities? Do you get the sense from your CE colleagues that it leans more in the direction of public relations or more in the direction of policy?

2. Which faculty members or representatives of other units on campus will you be dealing with? What can you learn from your CE colleagues about these individuals' history of involvement with, or their attitudes toward, continuing education? Listen, but remain open until you have had a chance to form your own opinions.

3. When preparing to meet with members of other units and faculties on campus, try to anticipate their concerns and reactions to, and their interest in, continuing education activities, and be prepared to address these.

Working with Administrative and Support Services on Campus

The university has been presented as a unique kind of organization. In fact, this discussion so far has been primarily concerned with the academic and professional units of the university.

As a continuing educator, you also will interact with representatives of various administrative and support units on campus. Which units this will be will depend on how functions are organized within your university and within your CEU, as well as on the particular requirements of your programs, but your contacts could include, among others, people responsible for:

We have been very successful in continuing education at the universities in doing a lot of things, but I think we still have a little bit of a journey in the way of expressing to our own institutions what it is we are doing. . . . I'm still surprised that a lot of people at the university do not know what we do or who we are (Robin).

- food services and catering

- room reservations

- graphic design and printing services

- media services

- campus security

- campus bookstore

- admissions
- student records
- counselling
- student aid
- campus parking
- libraries
- computer services
- public relations.

It is possible that you will work indirectly with the units responsible for many of these functions. There may be, for example, someone within your CEU who handles room bookings or audio-visual equipment requests. Obviously, this is the first thing that you need to find out—given all the tasks that must be performed, who has responsibility for what?

In dealing with various administrative and support services of the university, you may discover that, at times, these units find it difficult to accommodate the special needs of part-time adult learners. Two reasons may account for this.

1. Many of the rules and regulations that apply to full-time students were devised without consideration of the needs of part-time adult learners.

2. Universities are geared to cope with regular day students, but they are not always prepared to provide the same level of service to occasional day students, evening students, weekend students, and students at a distance.

The potential problems are too numerous to detail but, for example, consider an on-campus, nondegree, Saturday seminar. Students and instructors arrive to one or more of the following (and this after you think you have done everything to ensure a smooth day): locked doors (building or classroom), promised but missing audio-visual equipment, overly cool (or overly hot) rooms, promised but missing coffee (or food services may not be available on weekends), no chalk for the blackboard (or pens for the white board), closed libraries and bookstores (and, of course, since photocopying machines tend to be located in these places, they are not accessible either),

I hate dealing with the bureaucracy, the paperwork—those kinds of things. The deadlines—students miss the deadline by one day and now they can't withdraw from a course. But [these problems] usually get worked out. I find people, in most cases, very understanding, but it just takes a lot of stroking and a lot of PR and reminding people in admissions and in other areas about the nature of our work. And in most cases, they're wonderful—after you've gone through that first grovelling stage. And I wish sometimes that I could just pick up the phone and say, "Faculty of Arts, this is the problem. Can you help?" without having to do that [grovelling] beforehand. That's one of the things that I get tired of (Toni).

You want to build rapport with the people you are working with so that they will trust that you are not going to abuse them by asking for unreasonable things. . . . You have to let them know that you expect them to do the best that they can do because you're going to do the best that you can do. But they have to have a face to put to a name. If all they see is a piece of paper with a scribbled signature, what sort of responsibility do they feel? (Blair)

I think that one of the things you need to find out about the institution where you are working is how much they care about adult learners. Because what I found out is that our university is not geared administratively for the kind of learning that we are carrying out. . . . One Saturday, the doors were all locked. . . . I could get the people into the building but I couldn't get into our session rooms. And I had a darn hard time finding out who to call. . . . We don't fit into the flow of our university. You have to find out where you fit there, and then you have to do some networking. And that's just trial and error. You've got to find out who the people are that you need to know—for example, as I've mentioned, with facilities. You need to find out some real names of real people that you can contact (Les).

If you want to shorten the life of a perfectionist, give him [or her] a job in continuing education (Sandy).

missing handout materials, a room that is too small (or too large), and on and on.

How can you prevent these problems from occurring? To be honest, you probably can't—at least, not all of them. Given the number of people that you must work with, and the detail required to run even a one-day seminar, hitches are to be expected and problems will occur. And, budget constraints mean that libraries, day cares, and other services available to regular students will be available on a limited basis, at best, to part-time adult learners.

To work successfully with support-services providers, experienced continuing educators offer the following simple advice.

- Get to know the people that you have to work with and depend upon.

- Remember that these units tend to operate in a bureaucratic mode. Find out what the policies and procedures are, what expectations these units have of you, and then conform to these as much as possible. Do not use continuing education's special status as an excuse for not complying with rules and procedures that, if you were well organized, you could follow.

    Expectations will vary with the kind of service, but as an example, consider booking audio-visual equipment for a seminar. How are you to requisition these services? Are there forms to be filled out? Are there costs associated with any services? What lead times are required? What if you decide to cancel an event?

- Anticipate problems. Using audio-visual equipment again as an example, what do you do if the equipment does not arrive, or if the instructor experiences problems with the equipment? If your event is after regular hours, is there an emergency number that you can call? If there is, remember to give this information to the instructor.

- Explain your needs and make no assumptions about the service provided. Until you have some experience, ask even obvious questions—you may be amazed by what you discover.

- If there are problems, sit down with the people involved.

38

Appreciate the constraints that they are facing and ask for their help in looking for creative solutions to problems that may recur.

- Assume, until proven beyond a reasonable doubt, that people are competent at what they do and that, like you, they want to do the best possible job.

- Remember to acknowledge and thank people for good service.

Most of the above is common sense and, clearly, it is not a prescription for avoiding all problems. The point is to avoid as many problems as possible and try to minimize the impact of those that inevitably do arise.

If there are administrative or support units internal to your CEU that handle the marketing, registration, or other functions, these same common-sense principles apply.

Questions to Ask

1. Make a list of the tasks that you know are part of your overall responsibilities within continuing education. Where a task involves contact with an administrative or support unit on campus, determine who is responsible for that contact—are you responsible? Is there someone within your unit who liaises with that administrative unit?

2. If you are responsible for liaising with campus administrative or support services, find out who the contact persons are in these units and make appointments to meet with them.

The Continuing Education Mission: More About the Philosophical Debate

In Chapter II, the purposes of adult education are examined and the philosophical debate within the field of adult education is described. How is this debate over purpose being played out within CEUs across the country? Educational programming may be the mandate of continuing education; however, increasing financial pressures, and the effects of these pressures on programming decisions, have created tensions among continuing

You know, the marketplace attitude which has been quite dominant in our field of practice for the last ten years or so poses some difficulties for those people who would like to keep students in mind, or the approach to the delivery of the service in mind, rather than the internal politics of our own little unit or our own little university. . . . I don't wish to give up those principles of adult education but, on the other hand, I recognize that you are working constantly, at best, within a mixed model (Robin).

There are only limited opportunities for ventures to make money so that you can do the things that you really think are important. . . . I think that you have to keep your eye on the bottom line because, as much as we might have high ideals and want to offer programs that respond to those ideals, we also have to make a living for the institution and, if we don't do that, we won't be here (Morgan).

. . . More and more it strikes me that we have to have a greater awareness of how we fit. . . . There is some glory in how we don't fit, and how we're on the edge and tangential and all that stuff. And there is a lot of value to that in a philosophical sense. But I think that in a really practical sense, given the conditions that universities are in right now, and will be for the foreseeable future, we have to be really aware of what we offer to the institution, and so it's important to have that grounding and that sense, and not just thinking that we are off doing our own thing (Ronnie).

It's very easy to put on courses for the business community that have a pragmatic orientation—"How to do what you want to do better." . . . We've got a lecture series [coming up] that looks like very pragmatic sorts of stuff, but the person who is doing this is going to be coming at this from a very critical approach, challenging assumptions about what is the role of western economies in Third World development. I don't know if we're going to have anyone after the first lecture, but I think that it is important for . . . business people to think about these issues (Jan).

educators over how this mandate should be achieved.

Continuing education has grown considerably in this country since the 1960s. Before this, the major focus of continuing education was on liberal and general studies. As the demand for professional continuing education and part-time degree study grew, so did the numbers of specialized continuing education units and the breadth of their programming. Kulich (1991) notes that over the last several decades, universities in Canada, compared to their European and British counterparts, have distinguished themselves in their broad provision of adult education programming.

At the same time, the growth and increasing domination of individualistic, market-driven programming—much of it geared to job-related needs—has caused concern among some continuing educators. This type of programming is supported by humanistic, learner-centred orientations, but its primacy also has been encouraged by funding arrangements that make most CEUs ever more dependent on tuition revenue. Unfortunately, assessments of what makes for important and worthwhile programming—both degree and nondegree—are narrowed, too often, to questions of marketability.

Even when a CEU's mission statement attempts to incorporate a pluralistic view of continuing education, current funding arrangements create a bias in favour of programming that has high revenue potential. Programs that serve broader social needs, such as public education programs on environmental issues, tend to have lower revenue potentials than programs directed at meeting individual needs. One unfortunate consequence is that programs with social purposes may be devalued and viewed as marginal by CEUs (Cruikshank, 1991).

To the extent that CEUs hire people who "fit" the market-driven approach—who, for example, are hired because they have marketing or consulting skills, or experience in industry training—programming for social purposes becomes even less salient to a CEU (Roberts, 1985).

For continuing educators who support adult education as a force for social change, the domination of market-driven programming designed to meet individual needs has created a philosophical dilemma. Some accept the financial arrangements imposed on continuing education and try to find ways to ensure that a portion of their programming addresses social concerns. This may entail, where the budget process allows, using gains in one program area to offset lower returns in another. In other cases, program planners look for external sources of funds to support low revenue programs, or they run programs knowing that the cancellation risk is high.

Other continuing educators, frustrated by what they see as a growing "education as business" approach to programming, particularly in the nondegree area, feel strongly that many of these programs are a "poor fit" with the overall mission of the university and its liberal traditions.[3] They argue that a good deal of continuing education programming is indistinguishable from the programs of non-university providers and that a reassessment of the continuing education mission is necessary, preferably before continuing educators are seen to be totally irrelevant by the university community. From this perspective, the question that needs to be clarified is "what is it that distinguishes university continuing education from the programs of other providers?"

This debate over the appropriate mission for continuing education has gained momentum during the last several years as universities, and CEUs, have come under increasing financial pressure. As more and more programming decisions are made on the basis of dollars and cents, the criticisms of those who are against using this standard as the sole criterion for programming are becoming louder. There appears to be a growing awareness among Canadian continuing educators about the importance of this issue and a willingness, despite difficult financial times, to look for ways to address this concern.[4]

If continuing educators agree with those who advocate a pluralistic and balanced approach to programming—one that

A lot more [adult educators] are viewing the kind of work that we do as a kind of business and that gets you into the philosophical side of education—education versus training and so on. People have to ultimately face up to those kinds of questions because, if they have a certain kind of outlook, then maybe they can do the kind of work that they want to do more effectively outside of a university environment (Pat).

"University continuing education provision in . . . Canada should, of course, contribute to access and to part-time degree opportunities for adults, and it should do so in partnership with other adult education providers. University adult educators must argue the case for opening up the university to greater continuing education and professional education. . . . But the universities must also be prepared to defend and extend lifelong learning which culturally enriches adult life and tests knowledge against experience and informs social action" (Spencer and McIlroy, 1991, p. 35).

---

[3]   These continuing educators would argue that the entrepreneurial model is inconsistent with the values and traditions of the university's academic model. See Chapter III for a description of the university as an organization.

[4]   The theme of the 1992 Canadian Association for University Continuing Education (CAUCE) Annual General Meeting and Conference was "The Continuing Educator: Entrepreneur or Social Activist?"; the 1991 Conference theme dealt with the role of continuing education in environmental education.

"... Those who practice continuing education are under enormous pressure to do that which is most expedient. Pressure comes from many sources: There is never enough financial support, space, or staff; the parent institution often has goals incongruent or different from those of the continuing education program; the community must be served as well as individual learners; and evaluation and accountability issues must be addressed. The practitioner finds him- or herself shifting priorities, juggling values, and skirting issues in order to maintain a program. If any philosophical issue guides the practice of continuing education, it is that of pragmatism—doing what is practical, what will accomplish desired results in as expedient a manner as possible" (Merriam, 1982, p. 89).

addresses individual and social needs, and one that is based on sound adult education philosophy (Cruikshank, 1991; Spencer and McIlroy, 1991; Campbell, 1984)—the challenge that continuing educators face is two-fold.

- Continuing educators must determine how education for social purposes can be encouraged and supported. This will not be easy given the current economic climate and the increasing pressure to be self-financing.

- Continuing educators must develop a more critical approach to thinking about practice. They need to be conscious about what they do and why they do it. Continuing educators must become "aware of the power of education and its politically charged nature" (Merriam and Caffarella, 1991, p. 282) and they must act in ways that attempt to address some of the current inequities in adult education.

Questions to Ask

1. Does your CEU have a mission statement? If yes, ask your CE colleagues or someone in a leadership position within your unit to explain how the unit tries to achieve the various goals within the mission statement.

2. After talking to CE colleagues, what can you conclude about the adult education philosophy that appears to characterize your CEU?

Suggested Readings

UNIVERSITIES AS ORGANIZATIONS

Blaney, J. P. "Cultural Conflict and Leadership in Extension." *Canadian Journal of University Continuing Education* 12,1 (1986): 70–78.

Campbell, D. *The New Majority: Adult Learners in the University.* Edmonton: The University of Alberta Press, 1984.

Clark, B. R. *The Higher Education System.* Berkeley: University of California Press, 1983.

PHILOSOPHY IN ADULT EDUCATION

See Suggested Readings, Chapter II, p. 21

Continuing Education Units in Canada

This section provides an overview of continuing education practice in Canada.[5] Clearly, the data given here does not describe any particular CEU, but it should help you to frame questions about your own CEU and how it functions.

The Structure of CEUs

1. Most universities report that they have a central administrative unit (a CEU) that operates continuing education programs. About half of these units report that they are primarily responsible for continuing education programming, while the other half indicate that they share this responsibility with faculties or academic departments.

2. The majority of CEUs report that they use advisory committees. Such committees serve a variety of purposes. Most often, advisory committees help formulate policy or they advise on the programs and services to be provided to learners and client groups. Representation on a committee depends on its nature, but faculty, CEU staff, part-time students, and business/community leaders are often included.

3. CEUs are organized in different ways but most have distinct programming and/or service areas. Most often reported were areas designated for summer session and distance education. Other commonly designated areas included business/commerce, second language education, fine arts/humanities,

This section is a "must read" if you have never been involved with CEUs before but you would like a "big picture" look at how CEUs are organized and how they tend to operate in Canadian universities.

---

[5] The information presented here is from a report published by the Canadian Association for Continuing Education (CAUCE). Entitled *Continuing Education in Canadian Universities: A Summary Report of Policies and Practices—1985* (Brooke and Morris, 1987), the report is based on survey data collected from 44 of 56 universities in Canada that, at the time of the study, were institutional members of CAUCE. The sample excluded most francophone universities in Quebec. Only selected data is presented here. Remember the small sample size when reviewing this data—the percentages can be misleading. For those who are interested, CAUCE is currently conducting a survey to update this information.

"In terms of major functions undertaken by the CEUs, the most frequently reported activity is the provision of university degree courses; this is followed closely by non-degree courses and university certificate programs. Found less frequently as a major function are research, community public relations and community development" (Brooke and Morris, 1987, p. 7).

counselling/advising, marketing, professional education, and community development.

4. Most CEUs have representation on senior academic decision-making bodies within their institutions.

5. The majority of CEUs report that their institutions have a formal mission statement that speaks to the importance of the continuing education function. The majority of CEUs report that they have their own mission or policy statements in addition to the institutional statements about continuing education.

CEU Personnel

1. The most common title for the head of the CEU is director (68 percent) or dean (21 percent). The majority of heads hold academic appointments, either within an academic department within their respective institutions (55 percent) or within the CEU (12 percent). About one-third of the heads do not hold an academic appointment. In 1985, half the heads reported that the highest level of formal education that they held was a doctorate, while about the same number reported a master's degree.

2. Second-level administrators go by a variety of titles, with associate or assistant director being most often reported. More than 50 percent do not hold academic rank within their institutions.

3. The number of personnel within CEUs varies considerably. A general classification of personnel consists of:

   • professional programming staff (with and without academic rank)

   • joint appointments of academic staff with other faculties, departments, or schools

   • professional instructional staff (with or without academic rank)

   • research staff (with and without academic rank)

   • technical staff

- support staff—who generally number two to every one professional programming staff person.

4. When asked how they spend their time, professional staff working in degree program areas responded somewhat differently than those working in nondegree program areas.

    - Whereas program development, implementation, and design accounted for 33 percent of the time of degree professional staff, these activities accounted for 52 percent of the time of nondegree professional staff.

    - Administrative activities accounted for 42 percent of the time of those in degree areas and 29 percent of the time of those in nondegree areas.

    - Time spent on marketing was about equal, with 13 percent for degree and 15 percent for nondegree areas.

    - Those in degree areas indicated that they spend about 8 percent of their time doing academic counselling, whereas this was a negligible activity among professionals working in nondegree areas.

    - Both those in degree and those in nondegree areas reported that academic pursuits, such as teaching, research, and writing, occupied about 4 percent of their time.

5. The majority of continuing educators, including the heads of CEUs, have no formal training in adult education. Many of those who do have degrees in adult education earned these degrees after entering the field (Bains, 1985).

Financing of CEUs

1. CEU funding comes from two major sources: a central budgetary allocation and tuition revenue. Only about 6 percent of all CEU funding is from provincial and federal government grants, foundations, and corporate allocations.

2. The funding pattern for any given CEU may be different, but of all funding received by CEUs, 50 percent comes from a central budgetary allocation and 44 percent comes from tuition (as reported in 1985).

"The perceptions prevailing among the respondents indicate that the staff of the CEUs feel that the senior administrators in their respective institutions fully recognize (for 16 per cent of the respondents) the importance of the continuing education program. Another fifty-four per cent feel that their senior administrators are generally supportive of the cause of the CEU, while 18 per cent stated that they have major reservations about the kind and amount of support provided by the senior university administrators" (Brooke and Morris, 1987, p. 10).

"The largest number of professional administrative programming staff for a single institution is 25 (with academic rank) and 32 (without academic rank). The largest number of research staff in a single CEU is 2 (with academic rank) and 4 (without academic rank). The largest number of technical staff in a single CEU is 27 and 110 for full-time support staff" (Brooke and Morris, 1987, p. 14).

Continuing Education Programs

Campbell (1984) classifies continuing education programs into five chief segments, reflecting a combination of content and purposes:

- part-time courses for university credit
- professional and paraprofessional studies
- liberal and general studies
- community development
- community services.

The courses offered by continuing education can also be classified in terms of the credentials that they provide. Courses are classified as being degree or nondegree, with the latter being further classified as certificate/diploma credit or noncredit. The terms credit and credit bearing are generally used to refer to degree courses; however, as the reference to "certificate credit" suggests, these terms are sometimes used to refer to nondegree courses that can be applied as credit toward certificate or diploma programs.

Courses are also classified in terms of the method of delivery. They may be offered on campus using traditional methods or they may be offered to students using distance education methods, the most common of which are off-campus delivery and correspondence.

The programming offered by CEUs across Canada varies considerably. Whereas some larger units offer the entire range of programming as depicted in the above classifications, others offer only degree or only nondegree programming. Most units offer some type of distance education delivery but the methods they employ vary.

Part-time Degree Studies[6]

As one of the fastest growing areas within adult education, it is not surprising that the majority of universities replying to the

---

[6] The information on degree programming is based on the responses of 33 institutions to the CAUCE survey; the information on nondegree programming is based on the responses of 36 institutions.

1985 CAUCE survey indicate that they offer part-time degree studies. The majority of CEUs that offer degree courses do so using distance delivery as well as on-campus delivery. In 1985, approximately 30 percent of the replying institutions indicated that they offered complete degree programs via distance education.

Generalizing about part-time degree studies, at this point, becomes difficult. There are differences between CEUs in a variety of areas.

- Responsibility for approving courses: Most often it belongs to the CEU, along with responsibility for scheduling courses.

- Program and course development: The vast majority of CEUs work in close co-operation with relevant faculty in offering degree credit courses. The majority of CEUs do not program in subject areas that are not taught in degree programs at their respective institutions.

- The definition of "part-time student": There is no common definition, although the most usual definition of a part-time student is one who takes fewer than 3.5 full courses during the academic year, or fewer than 2 full courses per term (34 percent). "Mature students" are generally defined as those who are twenty-one years of age or older.

- Orientation programs: Most CEUs offer some type of orientation program to part-time adult students. Typically, these programs involve features like academic advising, counselling, library orientation, study-skills seminar, writing skills, time management, and an orientation to the campus.

- Counselling and advisement: A majority of universities provide program advisement, career counselling, and personal counselling to adult learners. While counselling and advisement are generally available to students through academic units and a university counselling centre, a majority of CEUs surveyed also provide counselling and advising services to part-time adult learners.

- Responsibility for approving instructors: Most often it resides with the faculty, department, or school.

- Instructor recruitment: Overall, 64 percent of instructors teaching for CEUs are regular full-time faculty.

- Part-time instructor development: The majority of CEUs indicated that funds are very limited for this purpose, but over half the survey respondents indicated that they held some type of professional development activity, most often meetings or intensive workshops.

- Instructor salary schedules: Salaries tend to be lower for part-time instructors than regular full-time faculty. In the majority of cases, salaries are determined by collective agreements or by senior university decision-making bodies.

- Funding degree operations: Normally there is either an operating budget from the university, where the expectation is that the funds will be recovered through tuition revenue and returned to the university, or the degree operation is totally subsidized by the university through an allocated operating budget. In a minority of institutions, CEUs are expected to recover costs on direct expenditures. Overall, 67 percent of the funding for degree programming comes from universities and 28 percent is generated from tuition fees.

- Admission policies: These tend to be set by university senate or other senior decision-making bodies and they vary widely. Over half the institutions surveyed indicated that admission policies for continuing education students do not differ from those of regular, full-time students. The most common admission requirements are related to age or high school academicstandards.

- Registration policies and procedures: These show no clear patterns although the majority of institutions allow registrations from students who are not enroled in a degree program. Most CEUs report that they get some kind of registration assistance from the university's registrar's office; however, the nature of the support differs from one institution to another.

- Advance standing provisions: The majority of institutions have some provisions awarding advance standing to transfer students.

• Tuition fees: These are generally determined by a senior university decision-making body, but they tend to be comparable for part-time and full-time students.

Nondegree Studies

If the policies and procedures of part-time degree studies show considerable variation across Canadian universities, the situation is just as complex in the case of nondegree studies. As with degree studies, the majority of universities responding to the 1985 CAUCE survey indicated that they offer nondegree programming. Although distance education delivery is used less often for nondegree than degree courses, over 60 percent of institutions that offer nondegree programs make at least some courses available at a distance. Face-to-face, off-campus delivery and correspondence are the methods most often used.

The 1985 CAUCE survey paints the following picture of nondegree programming across Canada.

• Responsibility for approving courses: The majority of CEUs have this authority and virtually all CEUs are responsible for scheduling nondegree courses.

• Program and course development: Whereas most CEUs indicated that they work co-operatively with relevant faculty to develop courses, a few units indicated that they have no working relationship with faculty or that they co-operate only occasionally. The vast majority of CEUs indicated that they program in subject areas that are not taught as part of the degree program offered at their institution.

• Orientation programs: Three-quarters of the CEUs report that they do not conduct orientation programs for nondegree students. CEUs that offer orientation programs tend to focus on counselling and study skills.

• Counselling and advisement: While the majority of CEUs provide program advisement for nondegree students, only about 30 percent of the institutions provide career counselling for nondegree learners and 17 percent provide personal counselling.

• Instructor approval: About one-third of the CEUs indicate that they are responsible for approving instructors, but in the majority of units, approval is done in consultation with the relevant academic unit.

- Instructor recruitment: Overall, about 23 percent of the instructors recruited to teach in nondegree programs are regular full-time faculty.

- Part-time instructor development: Resources are limited for the professional development of part-time instructors. Forty-seven percent of CEUs indicated that they provide some instructor development activities for nondegree instructors.

- Instructor salary schedules: In terms of who is responsible for setting nondegree salary schedules, there are no clear patterns, but in 39 percent of institutions, salary schedules are set by the CEU head. In 1985, the average rate of pay was $43.00 per contact hour (the range was $20.00 to $100.00 per contact hour).

- Funding nondegree operations: In 1985, the majority of CEUs received an operating budget from their respective universities on the understanding that the funds would be recovered through tuition revenues. More often than is the case with degree programs, 29 percent of nondegree programs were required to recover costs on direct expenditures (most often including promotion, instruction, and staff time). Overall, 18 percent of the funding for nondegree programming comes from universities and 88 percent of the funding is generated from tuition fees.

- Registration: In the vast majority of institutions, the CEU is entirely responsible for handling nondegree registrations.

- Tuition fees: In 1985, nondegree fees varied considerably, from $4.80 per contact hour for hobby and recreation courses to $10.57 per contact hour for some seminars.

Questions to Ask

1. Based on the information in the CAUCE survey, draft a list of questions that you cannot answer about the structure and

functioning of your CEU. Determine who in your CEU can provide answers to your questions and make appointments to see these individuals.

A Word About Certificate and Diploma Programs

Like degree programs, nondegree certificate and diploma programs provide those who successfully complete stated program requirements with some type of credential—some testimonial to their learning in a defined sphere of knowledge or practice. Beyond this, there is little agreement in either the literature, or in university practice, about how these program types are to be defined (Holt and Lopos, 1991; Waalen and Wilson, 1991).

Diversity exists not only in the criteria and practices associated with certificates and diplomas, but also in terms of jurisdictional control. Waalen and Wilson (1991) determined that less than 20 percent of certificates are controlled by CEUs. The majority are controlled by academic departments, professional associations, and other external organizations. CEUs are involved in a management capacity with approximately two-thirds of these non-CEU programs.

While it is apparent that certificate programs are an important component of continuing education programming—in 1990, over 600 certificates were offered by 43 Canadian universities—it is also true that the certificate format is more important to some CEUs than to others. Less than 20 percent of universities offer over 50 percent of the certificates. The average number of certificate programs offered by an institution was 12. The actual number of certificates offered by given institutions ranged from a low of zero to a high of 81 certificates (Waalen and Wilson, 1991).

"...Certificates may be awarded for anything from an eight-hour presentation to several years of study. They may at one extreme certify mere attendance and at the other extreme a high level of academic achievement. The diploma is principally a generic term normally presupposing academic qualifications such as an undergraduate degree" (Waalen and Wilson, 1991, p. 3).

Questions to Ask

1. Does your CEU offer any certificate/diploma programs? How does your CEU define a certificate/diploma program?

2. What types of certificates/diplomas are offered?
   - Are they made up of degree courses, nondegree courses, or a combination?

- Are they offered as undergraduate, graduate, or professional development programs?

- Are there different levels within certificate programs (i.e., introductory, intermediate, advanced)?

3. What is the approval process for certificate/diploma programs?

4. What responsibilities does your CEU have for certificate/diploma programs? What are the responsibilities of other university faculties and departments, or non-university organizations? Responsibilities may vary with particular certificates/diplomas.

Suggested Readings

Brooke, W. M., and J. F. Morris. *Continuing Education in Canadian Universities: A Summary Report of Policies and Practices—1985.* Ottawa: Canadian Association for University Continuing Education, 1987.

Holt, M.E., and G.L. Lopos, eds. *Perspectives on Educational Certificate Programs.* New Directions for Adult and Continuing Education, edited by R. G. Brockett and A. B. Knox, no. 52. San Francisco: Jossey-Bass, 1991.

Waalen, J., and L. Wilson. *Policies and Practices in Certificate and Diploma Education in Canadian Universities: Final Report.* Toronto: Ryerson Polytechnic Institute, 1991.

Chapter IV

Adult Learners

Who Participates in Adult Education—and Why?

Answers to the question "Who participates in adult education?" depend significantly on how variables like *adult*[1] and *participation* are defined. A national study conducted in 1983 found that about 20 percent of the Canadian population aged seventeen years or over took an adult education course during that year (Devereaux, 1984). Participation was defined in terms of "all organized educational activities" (p. 1), but it did not include self-directed learning projects.

When self-directed or independent learning projects are included, participation rates increase dramatically. Allan Tough (1971, 1978), a Canadian adult educator, conducted a study in the early 1970s that has had a major influence on research and practice in North America. Tough discovered that about 90 percent of adults are involved in carrying out learning projects of their own design, independent of any provider. Tough defined learning projects as involving at least seven hours of the

This section is a "must read" if you think that the best reason for supporting adult education is because it serves those who have the greatest need for education in our society.

---

[1] The concept of adult is discussed in Chapter I.

[New continuing educators] need to be aware of the audiences that we serve and they need to be aware of adult learners' characteristics. I think that is a really important component. Who are our learners? (Gerry)

individual's time over a six-month period where the intention to learn accounted for more than half of the person's motivation. The average individual, Tough determined, engaged in eight distinct projects every year.

For the sake of clarity, participation, as it is used here, refers to involvement in educational activities planned by others, including CEUs, and not to involvement in independent learning projects. As a concept, however, adult education includes involvement in independent learning projects.[2]

Tough's findings illustrate how dynamic and pervasive adult learning tends to be in our society. They reinforce the notion that most adult learning occurs outside institutional settings. But Tough's findings also raise questions.

1. What characteristics distinguish those who participate from those who do not?

2. Since participation is largely voluntary, why do some people choose to participate while others do not?

Who Participates in Adult Education?

In general, participation research in Canada (CAAE, 1982; Devereaux, 1984) and the United States (Johnstone and Rivera, 1965; Cross, 1979; Darkenwald and Merriam, 1982) demonstrates that adult education has elitist qualities. Participation rates tend to be significantly lower for those with less than high school education, for those with low family incomes, for the unemployed, for the elderly, and for visible minorities. Explanations for this skewed participation have been related to the cost of education and other barriers and to sociocultural forces that bias participation rates.

It is important to understand what kinds of people attend different programs. You've got university prep people who are primarily mature people coming back to university. They may be working or they may be women re-entering the workforce who aren't working. Mostly, they are probably working, they have families, and they are probably up to here with commitments and responsibilities. . . . They want credentials, whether it's a certificate or a degree or a letter saying they completed a computer skills course (Jan).

Motivations for Participation

Understanding motivations for participation in adult education has interested theorists since Houle's (1961) influential typology of "motivational orientations" appeared thirty years ago.

---

2   For a definition of adult education, see Chapter I.

Based on in-depth interviews with active adult learners, Houle concluded that adult learners could be classified as:

- goal-oriented

- learning-oriented

- activity-oriented.

For example, adults might be motivated to take courses because they want to improve their job prospects (goal-oriented), because they want to learn more about particular subjects (learning-oriented), or because they want to do something "productive" with their evenings (activity-oriented). Houle's typology has stimulated considerable research (see, for example, Boshier's [1971] work with the Education Participation Scale; Boshier and Collins, 1985), but Houle's simple typology continues to capture the essence of research findings in the area of motivation (Brookfield, 1986).

Of course, things are never quite as simple as a typology would suggest. Regardless of the subject matter or the setting, adults appear to participate in educational activities for multiple reasons, with one reason generally dominating. A consistent finding of this research is that the single, most important reason for participating in adult education relates to the performance of everyday "tasks and obligations" (Johnstone and Rivera, 1965), particularly those related to work (Darkenwald and Merriam, 1982). The data from a national Canadian study on participation in adult education support this finding.

I think the whole what I call adult education part-time culture is something that I think people should be exposed to and that is, who are the people that we are dealing with, what are their motivations, how do they relate to each other, what are they looking for, how do they view knowledge, what do they want to do? (Pat)

Participants in adult education by type of course (1983).*

Type of Course	%
Job-related	42
Personal Development/General Interest	22
Hobby/Craft/Recreation	19
Academic	14
Other	2
Don't Know/Not Stated	1

* Adapted from Devereaux, 1984, p. 23. Used with the permission of the Secretary of State and the Minister of Supply and Services Canada, 1993.

The implication is that adults engage in learning to enhance their proficiency in performing adult life roles and tasks. Adults want education to be practical and applicable to the circumstances of their lives (Knox, 1986).

Barriers to Participation

As important as motivation is to understanding participation, it has not been very useful in predicting participation. In other words, knowing why people do participate has not helped to explain why many adults, with similar needs, do not (Merriam and Caffarella, 1991). To attempt to answer this question, researchers have also looked at those who do not participate and the barriers that might account for nonparticipation. Research into barriers suggests that there are at least three types.

- Situational barriers: These relate to an individual's particular circumstances at a given time.

- Dispositional barriers: These relate to the individual's attitude toward self and learning.

- Institutional barriers: These relate to policies and procedures of the institution that make participation difficult or impossible (Cross, 1981).

Individuals may not have the money to participate in adult education (situational barrier), they may be afraid of failure (dispositional barrier), or they may lack the necessary admission criteria (institutional barrier).

Other research, supportive of Cross's typology, has led to the development of a "Deterrents to Participation Scale" (Scanlan and Darkenwald, 1984; Darkenwald and Valentine, 1985) that has been used to identify several factors related to nonparticipation, including:

- lack of self-confidence

- lack of perceived relevance of available courses

- low interest in organized education

- personal and family problems

- cost of education

- lack of support and encouragement.

The Sociology of Participation

Most participation studies are based on why people say they do and do not participate; however, some researchers have taken a different approach and have analyzed participation using a sociological perspective (Jarvis, 1985; Quigley, 1990). In this kind of analysis, individual motivation is important, but so are factors related to the individual's position in the social structure. The individual may not be aware of these structural factors but they serve to constrain his or her ability to participate in adult education.

According to Jarvis, formal education, since it is part of the prevailing social system, exists to maintain that system. To this end, adult education serves a number of functions that help to explain why some people participate and others do not. For example, education exists to reproduce existing social relationships and to transmit the dominant culture. Since adult education is organized by those in the middle class, its content is middle class, its language is middle class, and it selects out middle-class participants.

Anyone coming into adult education needs good interpersonal skills. You are not dealing with someone who is eighteen or nineteen years old. You are dealing with an adult learner and someone who may be really scared about coming to the university for the first time, or the first time in twenty years (Chris).

Improving Access to Adult Education

Understanding motivations and barriers to participation has obvious practice implications for continuing educators. Knowing why adults participate in adult education helps to ensure that programs are relevant and attractive to adult learners. Similarly, an understanding of institutional barriers, the only barriers that are subject to control by continuing educators, is important if continuing education is to become more accessible to adult learners.

The concept of access has at least two dimensions for continuing educators. Continuing educators have been very successful in terms of small "a" access—that is, making the university more accessible to those adults who, in terms of their personal

One of the most important things that I do in my position is to look for gaps in services, for things that are important to adult learners who are considering a return or coming to university. . . . Where are we missing the mark? . . . In a lot of cases, we know what the issues are but it is difficult to put something in place, like child care, and make it financially viable (Ronnie).

characteristics, are similar to continuing education's existing constituency. Developments in distance education, for example, have removed traditional geographic barriers to university education. Continuing educators, notwithstanding some very good programs, have been less successful in encouraging big "A" Access—that is, making the university accessible to nontraditional participants including Aboriginal people, the poor, the elderly, and those with limited educational preparation. Sociological interpretations of the functions of adult education provide insight into why this challenge has been so difficult to meet. For information and insight into the needs of culturally diverse groups, refer to the suggested readings at the end of this section.

Questions to Ask

1. What demographic/motivational data is available on the adult learners who participate in programs for which you have some responsibility? Can you construct a student profile for each program?

2. What kinds of "client services" does your CEU or your university make available to adult learners? What barriers do these services address? Where are the gaps in services?

Suggested Readings

PARTICIPATION DATA

Canadian Association for Adult Education. *From the Adult's Point of View*. Toronto: Canadian Association for Adult Education, 1982.

Devereaux, M. S. *One in Every Five: A Survey of Adult Education in Canada*. Ottawa: Statistics Canada and Education Support Sector, Department of the Secretary of State, 1984.

Tough, A. *The Adult's Learning Projects: A Fresh Approach to Theory and Practice in Adult Learning*. Toronto: Ontario Institute for Studies in Education, 1971.

Motivation/Barriers to Participation

Houle, C. O. *The Inquiring Mind.* Madison: University of Wisconsin Press, 1961.

Jarvis, P. *The Sociology of Adult and Continuing Education.* London: Croom Helm, 1985.

Scanlan, C. S., and G. G. Darkenwald. "Identifying Deterrents to Participation in Continuing Education." *Adult Education Quarterly 34,* 3 (1984): 155–66.

Cultural Diversity

Cassara, B. B., ed. *Adult Education in a Multicultural Society.* London: Routledge, 1990.

Culleton, B. *In Search of April Raintree.* Winnipeg, MB: Pemmican, 1983.

Ross-Gordon, J. M.; L. G. Martin; and D. Buck Briscoe. *Serving Culturally Diverse Populations.* New Directions for Adult and Continuing Education, no. 48. San Francisco: Jossey-Bass, 1990.

Adult Development and Learning

As with most topics covered in this manual, none of these "mountain tops" receives much more that a cursory nod. You are encouraged to read selections from the suggested readings that follow this section before drawing any conclusions about this material.

Adult Development

The importance of learning in adulthood, and the preferences adults demonstrate for learning activities related to adult responsibilities, has focused considerable attention on the con-

This section is a "must read" if you are a "closet believer" in the notion that most significant learning probably occurs in childhood.

"Learning can be thought of as a process by which behavior changes as a result of experiences" (Maples and Webster, as quoted in Merriam and Caffarella, 1991, p. 124).

cept of adult development (Bee, 1987; Merriam and Caffarella, 1991). What is missing from this impressive body of theory and research is a general consensus about what adult development is and what goals it serves. While some theorists see adult development in terms of linear, sequential stages (Erikson, 1982), and sometimes age-specific (Levinson, 1986), others see developmental needs as stemming from the tasks and social roles that adults perform or from the particular events that mark their lives (Havighurst, 1972; Brim and Ryff, 1980).

Some theorists define adult development in terms of an ultimate end, such as self-actualization (Maslow, 1970). For others, adult development has no specific end or necessary outcome (Tennant, 1988). Development implies "change," but it need not be related to the idea of "growth." Change can be viewed neutrally or even negatively (Bee, 1987).

More recently, long accepted humanistic notions that autonomy and independence are characteristics of fully developed adults, at least in our society, have come under scrutiny. Critical of the methodologies used in much developmental research, theorists such as Gilligan (1982) argue that connectedness and interdependence are important to female development. Studies such as these are forcing theorists to reconsider and broaden conceptions of adulthood.

What is Meant by "Learning"?

Learning has been defined in many ways. Traditionally, psychologists viewed learning as an *outcome,* as a change in behaviour. This definition is problematic in that it does not incorporate learning that, for whatever reasons, is not acted upon. Currently, most definitions of learning include the idea that learning can involve potential change. Consider the following definition:

> Learning is a relatively permanent change in behavior or in behavioral potentiality that results from experience and cannot be attributed to temporary body states such as those induced by illness, fatigue, or drugs (Hergenhahn, 1988, p. 7)

Learning Theories

Unfortunately, the literature on learning is voluminous, fragmented, and difficult, at times, to organize for purposes of discussion. In reviewing theories about learning, it should be remembered that no single theory offers an adequate explanation of this very complex phenomenon. On the other hand, each provides a framework for interpreting examples of learning and each suggests solutions for practical problems that adult educators may face in program planning or as teachers or counsellors of adults (Merriam and Caffarella, 1991).

Learning as a *process,* rather than an outcome, focuses on what actually happens when learning takes place. Theories that attempt to explain the learning process are referred to as learning theories. Chapter II discusses adult education philosophy and introduces several general theories of learning. You may recall from that chapter that each philosophical approach has something to say about how adults learn and about appropriate methods and content for adult education. Each philosophical tradition, then, is based on a theory about the processes involved in learning.

One classification of general learning theories groups them into four major orientations (Merriam and Caffarella, 1991):

- the behaviorist orientation

- the cognitive orientation

- the humanist orientation

- the social learning orientation.

Attempts to develop learning theories applicable to adults generally draw their basic assumptions about learning from one of these orientations. A summary of the key characteristics of each orientation is presented in the Appendix.

Learning Styles

There is no common definition of learning style and no single theory on which the concept is based. Smith defines learning style as "the individual's characteristic ways of processing

When you start to see the lights come on in people's eyes, when you know that it is starting to click, you really start to feel good as a teacher. And I learned by practice how to become a teacher . . . you have to come at everything from at least three different angles. You have to use lots of approaches and examples and analogies so that people can link into one of them (Blair).

There can be few intellectual quests that, for educators and trainers of adults, assume so much importance and yet contain so little promise of successful completion as the search for a general theory of adult learning (Brookfield, 1986, p. 25).

information, feeling, and behaving in learning situations" (1982, p. 24). Essentially, people make sense out of, and attend to, their environments in different ways. As such, learning styles affect how individuals learn and they must be considered in the design of any educational activity. For example, research demonstrates that people fall on a continuum in terms of how they perceive their environment. Some people approach their environment in very specific, analytical ways (field-independent), whereas others tend to prefer a global approach (field-dependent). These differences have implications for the amount of structure, feedback, and direction that learners prefer in learning situations—greater, in all cases, for field-dependent learners.

Smith notes that learning styles have cognitive dimensions (as with field dependence/independence), affective dimensions, and environmental dimensions. Persistence in trying to learn something new, as an affective factor, varies considerably among individuals and persistence appears to be related to expectations of success. Environmental factors, like noise, temperature, and lighting, also differentially affect how people learn.

Physical Aging and Learning

The aging process, as most of us know too well, is accompanied by major physiological changes. What is less clear is how these changes affect our ability to learn. In general, and in the absence of underlying disease processes, most physiological changes do not appear to have a major impact on an individual's ability to learn (Bee, 1987; Merriam and Caffarella, 1991). Many of the problems that tend to accompany aging, including vision and hearing loss, can be corrected or the learning environment can be adjusted to compensate for these difficulties. One finding that has implications for planning programs for older adults is that reaction time tends to slow as an individual ages. The pacing of educational activities may need to be adjusted for older adults.

The relationship between age and intelligence has generated considerable controversy; however, current thinking suggests that adult intelligence is relatively stable until the sixth or seventh decade of life (Merriam and Caffarella, 1991). Where there is decline, it appears to affect an individual's ability at the "more difficult levels of functioning" (p. 156) rather than in the average ranges of intellectual functioning.

One difficulty with existing measures of intelligence is that they focus on academic ability. Research suggests that there are other dimensions of intelligence that are relevant to understanding and measuring intellectual ability in adults. Some argue, for example, that practical knowledge, based on experience and used in everyday problem solving, is an important component of adult intelligence (Sternberg, 1985, 1990).

I'm really happy working with adults and I like the idea of someone who has had a life outside the university and who can come and bring that to it. It's just a wonderful sharing experience (Toni).

Andragogy: Toward a Theory of Adult Learning

Chapter II discusses philosophies of adult education and suggests how different adult educators have looked at adult learning. As that discussion and the above statements on learning theories suggest, there is no general theory about adult learning. However, there have been several attempts to construct theories of adult learning, and without doubt, the most influential of these comes from Malcolm Knowles.

Influenced by humanism and the writings of Carl Rogers, Knowles's conception of andragogy, or the "art and science of helping adults learn" (1980, p. 43), makes four assumptions about the characteristics of adult learners.

1. As adults mature, their self-concept moves from one of being a dependent personality toward being a self-directed human being.

2. They accumulate a growing reservoir of experience that becomes an increasingly rich resource for learning.

3. Their readiness to learn becomes oriented increasingly to the developmental tasks of their social roles.

4. Their time perspective changes from one of postponed application of knowledge to immediacy of application and, accordingly, their orientation toward learning shifts from being subject-centred to being performance or problem-centred (1980, p. 44–45).

. . . Imagine this: You set up a course for adults in a standard high school and you set it for 9:00 in the morning when there are thousands of high school students all over the place. And these adults have to creep in amongst this absolute foreign culture to get to their class. Set the class half an hour later, the halls are clear, and adults feel comfortable. That kind of sensitivity to the audience is really important (Francis).

"Walking to the school from the subway, I was thinking about how many thousands of people all over the city, or the province for that matter, might be doing just what I'm doing—walking to school at 7:00 [p.m.]; me to register, they to their class. It's not that I expected a band or carnival or anything like that to welcome me at the front door, but I certainly didn't expect the front door to be locked! The grounds and drive-way were no festival of lights either. They were dimly lit and there was a stealthy, secret, almost mysterious quality to the atmosphere around that school. I didn't exactly feel like an intruder, but I didn't feel particularly welcome either" (Stabler, 1972, p. 6).

Based on these assumptions, Knowles draws a number of conclusions about how adult education programs are to be designed, implemented, and evaluated. Some of Knowles's implications for practice are listed below.

1. The learning climate: Both the physical and the psychological environment of learning should be constructed to make adults feel physically comfortable and at ease and psychologically accepted, respected, and supported.

2. Diagnosis of needs: Since an adult's need for self-direction is in direct conflict with the traditional, directive role of the teacher, adults need to be involved in the diagnosis of their own needs for learning. Knowles suggests that facilitators: (a) construct a model of the competencies or characteristics required to achieve a given ideal of performance; (b) help learners assess their present level of competencies in light of the model; and (c) help learners to measure the gaps between their present competencies and those required by the model.

3. The planning process: Learners should be involved in the process of planning their own learning with the facilitator acting as a guide and a resource person.

4. Conducting learning experiences: The learning-teaching transaction is a mutual responsibility of learners and teachers. The teacher's role is redefined as facilitator, guide, catalyst, and resource person.

5. Evaluation of learning: Since the ultimate sign of disrespect for an adult is to be judged by someone else, learners should be involved in a process of self-evaluation. Teachers help learners to assess the progress they are making toward their educational goals. Evaluation is a process of assisting learners in the re-diagnosis of learning needs.

6. Emphasis on experiential techniques: Experience makes adults a rich resource for learning; instructional methods that draw on learners' experience should be used—for example, group discussion, the case method, critical-incident exercises, role playing, skill-practice exercises, and simulation.

7. Emphasis on practical application: Adults should be as-

sisted to relate learning experiences to their life-situations.

8. Unfreezing and learning to learn from experience: Adults should be assisted to free their minds of preconceptions and to reflect on and learn from their experiences (1980, p. 46–51).

Knowles's concept of andragogy has been criticized on many grounds (Hartree, 1984; Brookfield, 1986; Pratt, 1988). Brookfield notes that many of the assumptions of andragogy have not been proven and that to assume that andragogy provides a model of good practice is questionable. A review of the few studies that do attempt to test the assumptions of andragogy has provided mixed results at best (Merriam and Caffarella, 1991). Brookfield (1986) questions three assumptions of andragogy and cautions practitioners about uncritically applying these to practice:

1. that self-direction is an inherent characteristic of adults

2. that adults are problem-centred

3. that learning should be focused on achieving competency and immediate application.

Adult educators may view self-direction as a desired outcome or goal of adult education, but there is little evidence to support the idea that self-direction is an inherent capacity of adults. The assumptions about problem-centredness and application, according to Brookfield, threaten to reduce adult education to task-oriented, instrumental learning.[3]

Despite these criticisms, andragogy has done more to shape the practice of North American adult education, and to give a sense of identity to adult educators, than any other writings in the field. It has made the adult learner the focus of adult education and, whatever its shortcomings, it continues to exert a powerful influence over adult education practice.

Of course, andragogy is not the only attempt that has been made to develop a theory of adult learning. Other theorists who have written about adult learning include Freire (1970), Cross (1981), Gilligan (1982), Knox (1986), Jarvis (1987), Schön (1983, 1987), and Mezirow (1991). For an overview of these works,

I was thinking about this [women's] program. We've got to get some prospective students on the [advisory] committee to know what is important and how it makes a difference. If I can help the learner bring in their perspective, I think that what I am doing might make a difference (Gerry).

"The teacher was holding up someone's picture and asking us what we liked or didn't like about it. Now this person was off to the side and behind me, so how could I talk to her about what I thought? Discussion in rows just ain't easy. . . . So the teacher was doing a lot of talking and then, after he finished his lengthy commentary, he'd ask if we agreed and was there anything else? I suppose that he'd learned that discussion meant asking questions. But the way he did it, there wasn't anything else to say" (Stabler, 1972, p. 8).

---

[3]   See Chapter II for a discussion of Behaviourism.

> *. . . [Adult educators] need to become more self-conscious learners themselves. [We need to be] not only reflective educators but reflective learners as well because I think that we have only got one subject, and that is ourselves, to work with, to experiment with, to study (Robin).*

refer to the Merriam and Caffarella text cited in the suggested readings that follow or to the original sources listed in the Bibliography.

Questions to Ask

1. What can you say about yourself as a learner? What do you know about your own learning style?

2. Make a list of the independent learning projects that you have engaged in over the past year or two.

Suggested Readings

REVIEWS OF ADULT DEVELOPMENT AND LEARNING THEORY

Bee, H. L. *The Journey of Adulthood.* New York: Macmillan, 1987.

Merriam, S. B., and R. S. Caffarella. *Learning in Adulthood.* San Francisco: Jossey-Bass, 1991.

LEARNING STYLES

Kolb, D. A. "Learning Styles and Disciplinary Differences." In *The Modern American College,* edited by A. W. Chickering and Associates, 232–55. San Francisco: Jossey-Bass, 1981.

Smith, R. M. *Learning How to Learn: Applied Theory for Adults.* New York: Cambridge, 1982.

ANDRAGOGY

Knowles, M. S. *The Modern Practice of Adult Education: From Pedagogy to Andragogy* (revised and updated). New York: Cambridge, 1980.

Facilitating Adult Learning

If theory is to guide practice, what are the principles of practice that are thought to result in meaningful adult learning experiences? What implications do these principles have for the design and facilitation of adult education programs? This section considers those ideas about adult learning and development that have had the greatest impact on adult education practice in North America.

Many of the principles of practice derive from humanistic orientations, but the influences of other traditions are apparent as well. These principles are evidenced in the writings of theorists like Brookfield (1986, 1987), Knowles (1980), Knox (1986), Mezirow (1984b, 1991), and Schön (1983, 1987). In general, they support the notion that an effective teaching and learning encounter involves a transaction between facilitators and learners that is "active, challenging, collaborative, critically reflective, and transforming" (Galbraith, 1991, p. 1). Adult education activities are learner-centred and democratic in that they encourage a free and open discussion of beliefs, values, and practices.

Brookfield (1986) identifies six principles of effective practice in facilitating adult learning. These principles apply to teaching-learning transactions as well as to the program planning functions of curriculum development and instructional design.

1. Participation in learning is voluntary; adults have the freedom to choose the educational activities in which they become involved.

2. Effective practice is characterized by respect for one another's self-worth; challenge and criticism are important to educational activities but they should not denigrate or embarrass participants.

3. Facilitation is collaborative and participatory; participants should be engaged in the process of diagnosing needs, setting objectives, determining curriculum and methodologies, and developing evaluation criteria and procedures.

4. Praxis, which involves a continual and collaborative process

This section is a "must read" if you have read the previous sections on adult participation and learning but are still confused about the conclusions adult educators draw from this research and how these conclusions affect practice.

One of the rules that [he] taught me, and I will always respect him for that, was "make sure that what you are doing is fair and best for the student, but make sure that it is also fair and best for other students so that you can live with that decision." Every time I made a decision in the first year in my position, he would challenge me, "Have you done these two steps?" (Toni)

I think that if we don't develop initially a very high respect for the people that we are dealing with as learners, then we are missing the core of what we are about. . . . One of the things that we need to be doing is to make sure that we are absolutely certain that [new continuing educators], as they embark upon their practice with adult learners, are highly sensitized to the kinds of pressures and needs and aspirations that part-time learners have. Sometimes we run across instructors who are extremely naive or cavalier about that (Pat).

of action and reflection on action, is central to effective facilitation.

5. An important goal of facilitation is to encourage critically reflective thinking; adults become aware that meaning is socially constructed, and by examining habitual ways of thinking and acting, they are encouraged to explore new ways of thinking and acting.

6. The aim of facilitation is to encourage self-directed, empowered adults; the essence of a successful teaching-learning transaction is to help adult learners assume increasing independence and responsibility for their own learning and subsequent actions.

Other writers have attempted to synthesize principles of practice from the literature on adult learning (Brundage and MacKeracher, 1980; Darkenwald and Merriam, 1982; Smith, 1982). These writings have all been influenced by the assumptions of andragogy. They share a belief in the diversity of adult learners—in their development, in their learning styles, and in their motivations for participation—and they recognize that this diversity must be considered in planning and conducting programs for adults.

After reviewing Brookfield's principles of practice and the writings of others, Galbraith (1991, p. 16) states that the following principles should guide teaching and learning, and the design and development of adult education programs.

1. *An appropriate philosophical orientation must guide the educational encounter.* The importance of philosophy to adult education practice is discussed at length in Chapter II. Since adult educators have considerable freedom to make decisions about educational activities—about what is taught, for what purposes, and to whom—they are also responsible for ensuring that their decisions are based on a coherent, integrated set of assumptions about adult education.

2. *The diversity of adult learners must be recognized and understood.* Knowles (1980) characterizes adults as self-directed, problem-centered, and with a high readiness to learn. Long (1990) suggests that this view of adults makes them

look like "super learners"—internally motivated, task-oriented, eager volunteers who exalt in learning. In reality, adult learners are a diverse and varied group. They have different needs and they are motivated to participate in education for different reasons. Physiologically, psychologically, and sociologically, adults are dissimilar. They enter the learning environment having experienced different roles, transitions, and crises. Too, adults bring different learning styles to the educational encounter. If learning activities are to be effective, they must be reasonably suited to the needs and characteristics of participants.

3. *A conducive psychosocial climate for learning must be created.* An effective learning environment is one where adult learners are physically comfortable as well as psychologically or emotionally at ease. The physical environment should invite participation—for example, the lighting should be adequate, the temperature appropriate, the tables and chairs adult-sized, and the room set-up suitable for the learning activities. The emotional climate should be responsive, supportive, challenging, friendly, and open without being threatening, boring, or patronizing (Knox, 1986). A positive emotional environment is one that is collaborative, that values and respects learners' input, and that challenges and invites challenge. Wlodkowski (1985, 1990) discusses a number of strategies that instructors can use to create a learning climate that enhances adults' motivation to learn. Instructors who are interesting in assessing their teaching style (i.e., teacher-centered versus collaborative) are referred to the Principles of Adult Learning Scale (PALS), developed by Conti (1985, 1990).

4. *Challenging teaching and learning interactions must occur.* Challenging teaching-learning transactions can assist adults to develop the skills necessary for critically reflective thinking. The first step in encouraging adults to consider alternative ways of thinking and acting is to challenge them to question their beliefs, assumptions, and behaviour. A number of teaching methods and approaches appear to be especially conducive to creating challenging teaching-learning transactions, including discussion, simulation, learning contracts, inquiry teams, case method, critical

One thing that strikes me about the literature on adult education . . . is that it tends to be too focused on what makes the adult so special in the educational milieu. I'm not sure, in practice, that many of us find a lot of that information to be really important. I think that what it really boils down to, essentially, is having common sense, being sensitive to the needs of the learner, no matter the age of the person (Morgan).

I think it is important to have some empathy for adult learners and an understanding of their situation. You don't have to bend the rules all over the place to accommodate them but you have to have an appreciation for someone who hasn't had any formal education since grade 12, has been working for fifteen years, and now they are coming back—and maybe they are upset and concerned (Rene).

incident, and mentoring (Galbraith and Zelenak, 1991).

5. *Critical reflection and "praxis" must be fostered.* Brookfield (1986) describes praxis as "a continual process of activity, collaborative analysis of activity, new activity, further reflection and collaborative analysis" (p. 10). Praxis and critical reflection foster the development of critical thinkers—individuals who are able to identify and challenge their assumptions, to imagine and explore alternative ways of thinking and acting, and to adopt an attitude of reflective skepticism that encourages ongoing learning (Brookfield, 1987).

6. *Independence must be encouraged.* Brookfield (1986) notes that independence in learning is as much an internal change of consciousness as it is the external management of the learning experience. Adults who are able to think critically are engaged in an ongoing, transformative learning process that increases their independence, self-directedness, and empowerment. Given the diversity that characterizes adulthood, one should expect that adults have different capacities for and move toward self-directedness at different rates. Guglielmino's (Guglielmino and Guglielmino, 1988) Self-Directed Learning Readiness Scale (SDLRS) associates self-directedness with eight factors: enjoyment of learning; self-concept as an effective independent learner; tolerance of risk, ambiguity, and complexity; creativity; view of learning as a lifelong, beneficial process; initiative and self-discipline in learning; awareness of learning needs and progress; and acceptance of responsibility for one's own learning.

Given the diverse settings and purposes of adult education, these principles may not be easy to implement; however, effective practice requires that they all be present to some degree.

These principles reflect the influences of humanism, progressive education, and radical education. They have implications for numerous aspects of continuing education practice: for program planning, implementation, and delivery; and for the roles of program planner, instructional designer, facilitator, counsellor, and administrator.

These philosophical underpinnings and the principles of

effective practice as outlined by Brookfield, and as restated by Galbraith, provide a framework for thinking about the areas of practice within continuing education, the focus of the next two chapters.

Suggested Readings

Brookfield, S. D. *Understanding and Facilitating Adult Learning.* San Francisco: Jossey-Bass, 1986.

Brundage, D. H., and D. MacKeracher. *Adult Learning Principles and Their Application to Program Planning.* Toronto: Ontario Ministry of Education, 1980.

Galbraith, M. W., ed. *Facilitating Adult Learning: A Transactional Process.* Malabar, Fl.: Robert E. Kreiger, 1991.

Chapter V

Continuing Education Practice

An Overview of Professional Functions

It is easier to talk about the functions performed by continuing educators than it is to talk about their specific positions. A glance at the *Canadian Association for University Continuing Education Handbook 1992* (CAUCE, 1992) indicates that the tasks performed by CEUs, the way these tasks are assigned to individuals, and the titles given to positions vary. These differences are due to factors like the size of the unit, its organization, its overall responsibilities within the university, and the content of its programming.

On the other hand, regardless of tasks or title, the work of continuing educators can be classified according to one or more of the following basic functions:

- program development

- administration

- counselling

- instruction (Darkenwald and Merriam, 1982).

This section is a "must read" if you are still confused about the kinds of work that continuing educators do.

The most important things that I do are all related to the programs that we currently have and the new programs that I am developing. In terms of the programs, . . . the issue for me is one of quality—are these programs meeting the needs of students, of employers? Are they satisfying the academic standard, whatever that is, of the institution? Are we doing a good job of what we say we are doing? Are we paying enough attention to what is being taught in the curriculum—the specific content in the course—and to what is going on in the classroom by way of the teaching? Are we paying attention to recruitment, the development and the ongoing supervision of instructors? . . . If these programs are doing well, that's fine, but we need to be looking to develop new areas all the time. That is something that should get more of my attention (Lee).

Program Development

The vast majority of full-time continuing educators have positions that require them to perform program development functions as their primary responsibility. Program development includes activities such as assessing needs, setting objectives, designing learning events and obtaining necessary resources, implementing and managing learning events, and evaluating outcomes.

A continuing educator's position may involve all or most of these activities, or it may focus on some aspect of the program development process. For example, in some CEUs, the administrative tasks involved in offering programs are assigned to positions with titles like program assistant, program manager, or program administrator. In distance education programming, the development of curriculum formats and educational materials may be assigned to instructional designers, while technical specialists may be required to manage the technologies used in delivering programs. Positions dedicated to marketing and public relations have also become increasingly common in CEUs in recent years. Whether a continuing educator is responsible for all facets of program development, or only parts of the process, it is important to have an understanding of the entire process, and how the various components relate to one another.

The program development process clearly involves an instructional component. In making decisions about what educational activities to offer, how to design these activities, and what kinds of instructional resources are required, program developers are involved in traditional instructional decisions. Too, responsibilities for staffing programs, orienting instructors, designing course materials, and evaluating the instructor's performance involve continuing educators in instructional issues. Program development, then, requires an understanding of adult learners and how adult learning can be facilitated.

There is also a substantial administrative component to program development. Considerable management and administrative skills are involved in making any program a reality. Skills in planning, budgeting, and time management, in organizing and conducting meetings, and, more generally, in interpersonal relations and communication, are all required as part of the program development process.

Continuing educators who perform functions related to program development, and who also have contact with adult learners, may discover that their positions also include a counselling component in the form of program advisement. Some knowledge of how to provide effective program advisement to adult learners is necessary for many who are involved in program development.

Administration

In discussing administration as a separate function, there is an attempt to distinguish between the work of deans, directors, and others who manage and administer the CEU and the administrative activities of program developers. In fact, this is not always an easy separation to make. Some traditional management concerns, like obtaining financial resources for programs and hiring, often fall under the program development function. Too, many continuing educators are involved in positions that require them to be both part-time administrators and program developers.

In this manual, we are concerned with administrative activities that relate to program development—for example, planning and staffing programs. Those activities that relate more broadly to the management and administration of the CEU, or to program areas within the CEU, fall outside the scope of this manual.

Instruction

For a minority of continuing educators, instructing adult learners is a primary function of their positions. More commonly, when continuing educators are involved in instruction, it is secondary to their other responsibilities.

Most people who instruct continuing education programs are hired on a part-time basis by the CEU. They may be faculty members who are hired on an overload basis, or in the case of nondegree programs, they are often individuals who are not professional educators but who are hired because of their specialized knowledge or expertise.

Counselling

Again, for a minority of continuing educators, counselling, either academic or personal, is a primary function of their positions. Until recently, the counselling function in continuing education was often associated with the needs of adult learners in particular programs. More recently, counselling positions are beginning to appear in CEUs as part of the general package of services available to adult learners. As with instructors of adults, few counsellors in continuing education have had training in adult education.

Since program development is the function that most continuing educators perform, it is discussed in additional detail in this and the next chapter. If you are interested in additional information on the administrative, instructional, and counselling functions of continuing educators, some suggested readings follow.

Suggested Readings

ADMINISTRATION OF CONTINUING EDUCATION

Freedman, L. *Quality in Continuing Education.* San Francisco: Jossey-Bass, 1987.

Simerly, R. G., ed. *Strategic Planning and Leadership in Continuing Education.* San Francisco: Jossey-Bass, 1987.

Smith, D. H., and M. J. Offerman. "The Management of Adult and Continuing Education." In *Handbook of Adult and Continuing Education,* edited by S. B. Merriam and P. M. Cunningham, 246–59. San Francisco: Jossey-Bass, 1989.

ADULT EDUCATION INSTRUCTION

Barer-Stein, T., and J. A. Draper, eds. *The Craft of Teaching Adults.* Toronto: OISE Press, 1988.

Brookfield, S. D. *The Skillful Teacher.* San Francisco: Jossey-Bass, 1990.

Hayes, E., ed. *Effective Teaching Styles.* New Directions for Continuing Education, no. 43. San Francisco: Jossey-Bass, 1989.

...can set up a series of ...ave tried to stay away, ...possible, from the "ad ...programming. In other ...eed to ask, "Why are we ...Whose need is it going ...ith what other program ...e some kind of continu- ...gration? What next? ...people want after this?"

...hat a lot of us use the ...ing and we don't know ...s to do planning—so we ...ng a lot of "one shot" ..."Great, this term is ...plan for the next term." ...planning is extremely ...n our field. Otherwise, ...we find ourselves with ...programs that have ma- ...ied and we haven't even ...e skills that are required ...are very very impor- ...should at least be aware ...bin).

...and I think that this is ...nt area for me, a lot of ...ogram ideas. That in- ...ning the environment ...at what I feel are some ...ome program directions ...s, that I feel that my ...should be looking at

Models of Program Development

The program development process is generally depicted as a series of steps or elements that, taken together, encompass all of the tasks and decisions necessary to design and implement adult education activities. In this section, we will consider three models of program development.

The following basic, six-step model of program development is offered by Sork and Caffarella (1989, p. 234):

1) analyze the planning context and the client system

2) assess needs

3) develop program objectives

4) formulate instructional plan

5) formulate administrative plan

6) design a program evaluation plan.

Sork and Caffarella refer to this model as a "basic" model because each step, in reality, incorporates a number of complex tasks and decisions. This brings us to several important points that must be made about program development models.

1. Models are prescriptive. They describe how planning should happen but not how it actually happens in practice.

2. Models are overly simplistic. Although most program development models have between five and ten fairly consistent steps or elements, planning is an extremely complex process that involves countless tasks and decisions—well, not exactly countless. In one study, nearly 130 separate programming tasks were identified (Burnham, 1988).

3. Models are often presented as involving linear steps. Although linear models are helpful in that they imply logic and a preferred ordering of elements, planning is a far more dynamic and interactive process than the models suggest. In fact, it is more likely that you will find yourself moving back and forth between tasks at different steps and working on a number of tasks at the same time. Too, information that you acquire quite late in the process may cause you to go back and modify decisions that you made during the initial planning stages.

Renner, P. F. *The Instructor's Survival Kit: A Handbook for Teachers of Adults*, 2d ed. Vancouver: Training Associates Ltd., 1983.

COUNSELLING ADULT LEARNERS

DiDilvestro, F. R., ed. *Advising and Counselling Adult Learners*. New Directions for Continuing Education, no. 10. San Francisco: Jossey-Bass, 1981.

Miller, J. V., and M. L. Musgrove, eds. *Issues in Adult Career Counselling*. New Directions for Continuing Education, no. 32. San Francisco: Jossey-Bass, 1986.

Schlossberg, N.; A. Lynch; and A. Chickering. *Improving Higher Education Environments for Adults*. San Francisco: Jossey-Bass, 1989.

Woolfe, R.; S. Murgatroyd; and S. Rhys. *Guidance and Counseling in Adult and Continuing Education*. Milton Keys: Open University Press, 1987.

Program Development

The practice of continuing education is synonymous with activities that lead to the creation and implementation of educational programs for adult learners—so synonymous, in fact, that continuing educators are sometimes referred to as "programmers."[1] This section looks at the concept of program development, examines some models that outline the program development process, and briefly considers several key elements in this process.

This section is a "must read" if you think that "programming" is just a computer term.

The Concept of Program

The concept of program has been used in many ways (Schroeder, 1970). Sometimes it is used in a narrow sense to refer to the

---

[1] This title tends to be identified with continuing educators who develop nondegree programs and who are involved in the broad range of activities associated with the program development process.

curriculum or what is taught in continuing education; at other times, it may be used to refer to all of the educational activities provided by an institution (i.e., the CEU's program).

For our purposes, the concept of program includes curriculum, but it is much broader than this. As suggested in the previous section, a program is the product or outcome of all of the activities that are involved in designing and implementing educational activities for adults. These activities include needs assessment and curriculum design, but they also include marketing, budgeting, and evaluation (Boyle, 1981).

Kowalski (1988) distinguishes between a comprehensive program, which refers to all of the adult education activities planned by an institution (e.g., a hospital), and an individual program, which refers to a component of a comprehensive program (e.g., a class in infant care). Knowles (1980, p. 222) makes a similar distinction between comprehensive programs and learning activities, the separate units or sequences of activity that make up comprehensive programs. Both theorists are drawing a distinction between *macro* and *micro* levels of program development. The process for planning and implementing programs at both levels is essentially the same, but as Kowalski notes:

> When planning is discussed, one should realize that the macro aspect is much more entangled and requires a myriad of inputs. The micro aspect is much more specific, and the task of planning is simplified by the narrowness of the activity (1988, p. 88).

The difference between planning at these two levels is illustrated by the process involved in planning a continuing management education program for a group of administrators. At the macro level, the outcome of the program development process might be a comprehensive, integrated program that includes a multi-level certificate program, an annual conference, a series of skill-building workshops, and a luncheon lecture series. Planning the component events, such as a workshop or a luncheon lecture, would involve micro-level planning. Generally, macro-level planning involves longer-range planning than planning at the micro level.

Planning Defined

Planning is a formalized procedure used to create continuing education programs. Boone (1985, p. 64) sees planning as being guided by certain assumptions.

- Planning is a futuristic activity.
- The planning behavior of the adult education organization is proactive rather than reactive.
- Planning enhances efficiency in the adult education organization.
- Planning is sequential or stepwise; it begins with the organization and its renewal process, continues through the sequential steps of the linkages process, and ends with an analysis of identified educational needs.
- Planning is collaborative; it involves representatives of all who are affected by it.

Four generic concepts undergird Boone's assumptions about planning.

- Planned change: Planning is directed toward achieving certain outcomes.
- Linkage: Planning involves linking adult education to other elements within the organization, to its environment, and to its adult learners.
- Democracy: Planning should be collaborative and participatory.
- Translation: Planning must involve clear communication of adult education values and objectives and the needs on which these objectives are based.

The Concept of Program Development

The terms program planning, program development, and programming are often used interchangeably by adult educators. Although some might argue that planning is more restrictive, for our purposes these terms are equivalent and they refer to the processes of planning and managing programs.

Renner, P. F. *The Instructor's Survival Kit: A Handbook for Teachers of Adults,* 2d ed. Vancouver: Training Associates Ltd., 1983.

COUNSELLING ADULT LEARNERS

DiDilvestro, F. R., ed. *Advising and Counselling Adult Learners.* New Directions for Continuing Education, no. 10. San Francisco: Jossey-Bass, 1981.

Miller, J. V., and M. L. Musgrove, eds. *Issues in Adult Career Counselling.* New Directions for Continuing Education, no. 32. San Francisco: Jossey-Bass, 1986.

Schlossberg, N.; A. Lynch; and A. Chickering. *Improving Higher Education Environments for Adults.* San Francisco: Jossey-Bass, 1989.

Woolfe, R.; S. Murgatroyd; and S. Rhys. *Guidance and Counseling in Adult and Continuing Education.* Milton Keys: Open University Press, 1987.

Program Development

The practice of continuing education is synonymous with activities that lead to the creation and implementation of educational programs for adult learners—so synonymous, in fact, that continuing educators are sometimes referred to as "programmers."[1] This section looks at the concept of program development, examines some models that outline the program development process, and briefly considers several key elements in this process.

This section is a "must read" if you think that "programming" is just a computer term.

The Concept of Program

The concept of program has been used in many ways (Schroeder, 1970). Sometimes it is used in a narrow sense to refer to the

---

[1]   This title tends to be identified with continuing educators who develop nondegree programs and who are involved in the broad range of activities associated with the program development process.

I think that it is really important to stay alert for new program opportunities. Sometimes people coming into this field aren't used to wearing a whole variety of hats at once and you have to always have your ears and your eyes open for new ideas and new opportunities and new liaisons that you can form with people (Morgan).

Another piece of advice that I would give [to new continuing educators] is that they need to plan out, both long term and short term, their jobs—what they need to do—and they need to constantly review and revise those plans (Shawn).

You always need to be looking for future, innovative projects. You need to be looking beyond the present day-to-day operations. If you don't do that, you are going to become stale. . . . Somehow, you have got to find a way to have that window of innovation as part of your responsibility (Dale).

curriculum or what is taught in continuing education; at other times, it may be used to refer to all of the educational activities provided by an institution (i.e., the CEU's program).

For our purposes, the concept of program includes curriculum, but it is much broader than this. As suggested in the previous section, a program is the product or outcome of all of the activities that are involved in designing and implementing educational activities for adults. These activities include needs assessment and curriculum design, but they also include marketing, budgeting, and evaluation (Boyle, 1981).

Kowalski (1988) distinguishes between a comprehensive program, which refers to all of the adult education activities planned by an institution (e.g., a hospital), and an individual program, which refers to a component of a comprehensive program (e.g., a class in infant care). Knowles (1980, p. 222) makes a similar distinction between comprehensive programs and learning activities, the separate units or sequences of activity that make up comprehensive programs. Both theorists are drawing a distinction between *macro* and *micro* levels of program development. The process for planning and implementing programs at both levels is essentially the same, but as Kowalski notes:

> When planning is discussed, one should realize that the macro aspect is much more entangled and requires a myriad of inputs. The micro aspect is much more specific, and the task of planning is simplified by the narrowness of the activity (1988, p. 88).

The difference between planning at these two levels is illustrated by the process involved in planning a continuing management education program for a group of administrators. At the macro level, the outcome of the program development process might be a comprehensive, integrated program that includes a multi-level certificate program, an annual conference, a series of skill-building workshops, and a luncheon lecture series. Planning the component events, such as a workshop or a luncheon lecture, would involve micro-level planning. Generally, macro-level planning involves longer-range planning than planning at the micro level.

Planning Defined

Planning is a formalized procedure used to create continuing education programs. Boone (1985, p. 64) sees planning as being guided by certain assumptions.

- Planning is a futuristic activity.

- The planning behavior of the adult education organization is proactive rather than reactive.

- Planning enhances efficiency in the adult education organization.

- Planning is sequential or stepwise; it begins with the organization and its renewal process, continues through the sequential steps of the linkages process, and ends with an analysis of identified educational needs.

- Planning is collaborative; it involves representatives of all who are affected by it.

Four generic concepts undergird Boone's assumptions about planning.

- Planned change: Planning is directed toward achieving certain outcomes.

- Linkage: Planning involves linking adult education to other elements within the organization, to its environment, and to its adult learners.

- Democracy: Planning should be collaborative and participatory.

- Translation: Planning must involve clear communication of adult education values and objectives and the needs on which these objectives are based.

There once was a teacher
Whose principal feature
Was hidden in quite an odd
    way.
    Students by millions
    Or possibly zillions
    Surrounded him all of
      the day.
When finally seen
By his scholarly dean
And asked how he managed
    the deed,
    He lifted three fingers
    And said, "All of you
      swingers
    Need only to follow my
      lead.
"To rise from a zero
To Big Campus Hero,
To answer these questions
    you'll strive:
    Where am I going,
    How shall I get there, and
    How will I know I've ar-
      rived?"

(Mager, 1984, p. i. Used by permission of Lake Publishing Company, Belmont, CA 94002, U.S.A. © 1984.)

The Concept of Program Development

The terms program planning, program development, and programming are often used interchangeably by adult educators. Although some might argue that planning is more restrictive, for our purposes these terms are equivalent and they refer to the processes of planning and managing programs.

Models of Program Development

The program development process is generally depicted as a series of steps or elements that, taken together, encompass all of the tasks and decisions necessary to design and implement adult education activities. In this section, we will consider three models of program development.

The following basic, six-step model of program development is offered by Sork and Caffarella (1989, p. 234):

1) analyze the planning context and the client system

2) assess needs

3) develop program objectives

4) formulate instructional plan

5) formulate administrative plan

6) design a program evaluation plan.

Sork and Caffarella refer to this model as a "basic" model because each step, in reality, incorporates a number of complex tasks and decisions. This brings us to several important points that must be made about program development models.

1. Models are prescriptive. They describe how planning should happen but not how it actually happens in practice.

2. Models are overly simplistic. Although most program development models have between five and ten fairly consistent steps or elements, planning is an extremely complex process that involves countless tasks and decisions—well, not exactly countless. In one study, nearly 130 separate programming tasks were identified (Burnham, 1988).

3. Models are often presented as involving linear steps. Although linear models are helpful in that they imply logic and a preferred ordering of elements, planning is a far more dynamic and interactive process than the models suggest. In fact, it is more likely that you will find yourself moving back and forth between tasks at different steps and working on a number of tasks at the same time. Too, information that you acquire quite late in the process may cause you to go back and modify decisions that you made during the initial planning stages.

Anybody can set up a series of lectures. I have tried to stay away, as much as possible, from the "ad hocery" of programming. In other words, we need to ask, "Why are we doing this? Whose need is it going to meet? With what other program can this have some kind of continuity or integration? What next? What would people want after this?" (Robin)

I think that a lot of us use the word planning and we don't know what it takes to do planning—so we end up doing a lot of "one shot" things—or, "Great, this term is over. Let's plan for the next term." Long-term planning is extremely important in our field. Otherwise, all of sudden we find ourselves with a couple of programs that have matured and died and we haven't even noticed. The skills that are required in planning are very very important and we should at least be aware of them (Robin).

I spend, and I think that this is an important area for me, a lot of time on program ideas. That involves scanning the environment and looking at what I feel are some new ideas, some program directions and thrusts, that I feel that my department should be looking at (Pat).

Recognizing that what actually happens in planning is often nonlinear, interactive models have been developed. For examples of these, see Nadler (1982), Simpson (1987), and Murk and Galbraith (1986).

4. Although the Sork and Caffarella model does suggest the importance of contextual factors to the program development process, many models place little or no emphasis on the way in which environmental, organizational, and personal factors influence the program development process. For example, the model of program development that follows from Knowles's concept of andragogy[2] makes no reference to the way in which contextual factors, such as the mission of the organization, impact upon decisions that are made during the course of program development.

In acknowledging the importance of contextual factors to program development, we are acknowledging something that every continuing educator knows—a continuing education program does not develop in a vacuum. Many factors impinge on and affect the program development process. The development of any program generally involves the input and collaboration of many people, and the role that these people play and the way in which the collaborative process is managed by the continuing educator will affect the program outcome.

In Chapter II, the point was made that the personal values and the philosophical assumptions of the continuing educator are important factors in shaping the development of adult education programming. Also important to program planning, and this is a point that is discussed in more detail later, is the experience in program development and the knowledge of the organization that the continuing educator brings to the planning process (Brookfield, 1986; Burnham, 1988; Dominick, 1990).

Kowalski (1988) identifies several other contextual factors that influence program development.

1. Environmental factors: In the case of continuing education, these would include factors that are external to the

---

[2] See Chapter IV for a discussion of the program development model implied by andragogy.

"[A model is] a simplified or idealized description or conception of a particular system, situation, or process that is put forward as the basis for calculations, predictions, or further investigation" (The Compact Oxford English Dictionary, 1991, p. 1,100).

The beauty of a model is that, at least if you have a model, you can modify it or change it or throw it away and start with something new. At least you know that you have got something to bounce [your ideas] off (Robin).

"A planning model is a tool used to help understand and bring order to a complex decision-making process. The typical planning model consist of a set of steps (which imply a preferred sequence or order to the planning process) or elements (which imply a more interactive or dynamic process) that suggest decisions that must be made and dependent relationships that exist between the various decisions. Any effort to summarize the complexities of planning—whether using steps or elements—is bound to oversimplify the process as it occurs in practice" (Sork and Caffarella, 1989, p. 234).

"... Professionals conduct their practice in the swamp of the real world, where problems do not present themselves as well-formed, unambiguous structures but rather as messy indeterminate situations" (Cervero, 1989, p. 109).

Program development, program evaluation, marketing—all of these are collaborative efforts where we work with other people. For example, program development—who is involved in that? Is it just the prerogative of [the continuing educator] working with one instructor, are we dealing with a whole [academic] department, are we dealing with an interdisciplinary group? Because each one of these [situations] will have its own nuances and at least an awareness of that would be useful (Robin).

I guess the hardest thing [about program development] is trying to make the best possible decision. Trying to weigh all the information . . . and never knowing if you've done all that you possibly could to develop the best possible program (Gerry).

university, such as the demand for the kind of adult education programming that continuing education can provide (e.g., continuing professional education, part-time degree studies, liberal and general studies, etc.), the attitudes of influential community members toward continuing education programming (e.g., employers or others who can provide financial support or reward participation), and the competition that continuing education may face from other providers who serve the same adult constituency. Clearly, environmental factors, such as intense competition from other providers, will place restrictions on the program plans of continuing educators.

2. The parent organization: Being situated within the context of the university, an organization that offers adult education as a secondary function, has important implications for continuing education programming. The nature of universities as organizations means that CEUs find themselves functioning in a somewhat unique context,[3] but one that can vary markedly from university to university. Some of the important variables that affect continuing education programming are listed as follows.

- The mission of the university: How important is continuing education to the mission of the university and what role is continuing education assigned?

- The mission of continuing education: What is the purpose of continuing education and to what degree does it exist to serve public needs for education versus organizational needs for financing or public relations?

- Resources: How are human, financial, and other resources allocated to continuing education?

- Governance: Since decision making within universities is extremely variable, to what degree does it constrain or encourage opportunities for continuing education?

- Program integration: To what degree are continuing education programs integrated with, or separate from, other programs of the university?

---

[3] For a discussion of universities as organizations, see Chapter III.

Organizational restrictions on continuing education programming can relate to any of these variables.

3. Planning factors: Numerous conditions, very specific to the planning process, can affect program development—for example, the quality of the relationships between those involved in the planning process, the adequacy of time lines given to planning, the availability of support staff time, and the experience of the program developer.

4. The program: The specific nature of the program affects program development decisions (e.g., a computer course on Lotus 1–2–3 versus a certificate program in counselling skills).

5. Adult learners: The program is affected by the adult learners who participate and who bring their own interests, values, and experiences to adult education activities.

Based on his analysis of the factors that affect program development, Kowalski (1988, p. 101) offers the following model for program development. Kowalski's arrangement of steps within this model emphasizes the importance of viewing program development as a cycle of activities that has no finite point as long as the program continues.

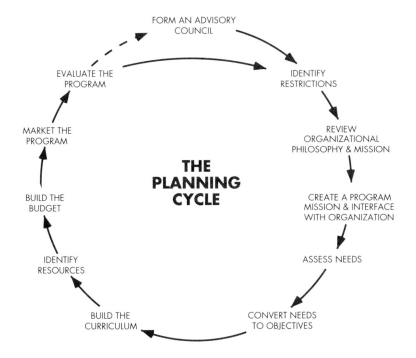

I read a lot of stuff on program planning and project management and they always do things so linear. It really drives me crazy because it doesn't work out that way (Les).

It is important to turn new [continuing educators'] attention, as quickly as possible, to learning about the context—the programs of the Division, its administrative systems, the staff, all of that. The new person has to be directed to go and do that. Maybe it's by reading the catalogues and promotion material, maybe it is by initiating a self-orientation process of walking around or making appointments and talking to people (Lee).

Another thing that drove me crazy during the first year was the . . . program. The time lines and the expectations that came down on us were unrealistic and . . . unreasonable. We realized that this wasn't even a Division issue, that this had come down from above the Division and there was really nothing that we could do about it. . . . And the personal cost was severe and the stress was high . . . you just simply grit your teeth, put your head down, and do it or do the best that you can in those circumstances (Shawn).

I don't want to put too much emphasis on one particular aspect or component of the process of program development as being the most important. What is important depends on where you are in the process. I think that we tend to think that things go from A to B in a nice sequential fashion and that is a misunderstanding of what we do. You have got one thing going here and one thing going there and they all have to come together at some point (Gerry).

Kowalski's model, and the model that follows, break down the Sork and Caffarella model into more detailed components.

The last model presented here is one that was developed by Lund and McGechaen (1981) for those working in community development. Although this model does not address all of the contextual issues discussed above, it is included because it provides a more detailed description of the tasks involved at each step of the development process—it's almost a checklist.

1. Assess community needs:

    • determine community structure

    • consult with community representatives

    • participate in community activities

    • conduct formal and informal research

    • identify community needs

    • determine priorities

2. Plan courses and programs:

    • prepare proposals

    • prepare budgets

    • advise on curriculum development or revision

    • obtain descriptions and outlines

    • locate facilities and schedule activities

    • recruit instructors

    • obtain supplies and equipment

    • develop instructional resources

3. Promote and market courses and programs:

    • identify target population

    • select advertising medium

    • prepare advertising

    • place and distribute advertising

    • conduct public relations

I would say to a new [continuing educator], give yourself a year. Don't expect to know what you are doing or to be tremendously productive and creative until you've been through the cycle. . . . There is a tremendous amount to learn and new people should not feel that they are going to make themselves look inferior by asking a lot of basic questions (Ronnie).

4. Manage courses and programs:

   - register participants

   - manage budgets

   - manage facilities

   - resolve complaints

   - manage administrative detail

5. Manage personnel:

   - orient instructors

   - facilitate instructor training

   - provide instructional support

   - relate to support staff

   - manage time and workload

6. Practise communication skills:

   - write reports

   - compile statistics

   - process forms

   - prepare correspondence

   - conduct interviews

   - perform advisory roles

   - communicate publicly

   - communicate interpersonally

7. Conduct evaluation:

   - evaluate programs

   - evaluate courses

   - evaluate instructors

   - conduct self-evaluation.

Find a mentor, find somebody that you can talk to. It may not be somebody in your area or your Division, although that would be the best, but at least find somebody that you can talk to about the field. . . . And, if it is not happening already, initiate meetings with people—with management, with your colleagues, even informal discussions with a support group . . . where you can ask questions and get feedback (Blair).

". . . Program development . . . is a process which does not lend itself to single solutions. Rather, each program presents the practitioner with a novel challenge which necessitates an understanding of the adult as learner, the environment as a restricting variable, and the parent organization as a controlling variable" (Kowalski, 1988, p. 10–11).

You have to have a lot of patience working with programs and learning how things operate. You need to have a sense of humour because sometimes things can get quite bogged down. . . . Don't jump too quickly. Sit back and watch things a little bit and understand what is going on before you act because, otherwise, you could alienate people within and without [the CEU] (Jean).

. . . Talk with experienced staff and talk with them often. So, it's not just visiting them for the first time and trying to get some idea of what they do but visiting them often. . . . Watch experienced staff. When you are at meetings, or in their presence, watch them and take note of what they do and how they do it. And new staff will quickly find out who the good models are. . . . I think that [new continuing educators] need to take the initiative to go along with [experienced staff] to the various kinds of experiences that they inevitably will be in. Ask an experienced staff person if they can go along to the advisory committees they are chairing or the evaluation planning committees they are involved in. This may be long before the new staff person has any program responsibilities or has the responsibility to conduct, call, or plan any of these activities (Lee).

My advice to a new [continuing educator] is to allow yourself to be imperfect. . . . There is no sense in getting uptight because yesterday we brought 3,000 pages of paper [to a course] but we forgot one. . . . And when you screw up, and we all do, you feel bad and you probably don't sleep well that night—know that everybody else is going to forget about it long before you do and, also, if you learn something from it, know that you won't feel bad forever. Don't let yourself get really bogged down (Les).

Documenting the Program Development Process

Another important aspect of program development, which is suggested by some of the tasks in the Lund and McGechaen model, is documentation. The process should be described in writing (i.e., what you did) and the outcomes of planning and management exercises should be written down (i.e., what you decided and the basis on which you made your decisions). Documentation provides legitimacy for your actions and historical records for those who come after you. Documentation is one of those administrative tasks that many continuing educators are loathe to perform, relying instead on minutes of advisory committee meetings and other secondary records that can provide, at best, only a partial record of the planning process. Take the time to document activities and you will likely discover several effective uses for these reports.

Becoming an Effective Program Developer

The complexity of program development can be daunting to those who are new to the experience, and while models are useful guidelines, they hardly prepare a continuing educator for the realities of practice. In fact, the simplicity of program development models may lead one to forget that each program development situation is unique, and that the outcome of the process will certainly be affected by conditions over which the continuing educator has limited control.

Learning to be an effective program developer under these conditions is not easy. If program development is situation specific, there can be no blueprints and recipes for practice. Models and other prescriptions for practice must be understood and interpreted within the context of your organization and in terms of the groups and individuals with whom you work. Expect that situations will arise that no program development model has ever alluded to, but that you will be required to handle decisively. Too, unless your organization offers a good orientation program, you will also need to determine how all the internal administrative systems operate—everything from how to ensure that instructors are paid to how to requisition supplies.

How should you go about trying to become an effective program developer? The advice from experienced continuing educators is to:

1) ask questions.

2) find out as much as you can about how your organization operates—who are the players and what are their interests and values? What are the administrative systems for getting work done both inside the CEU and around the university?

3) find a mentor, some role models, a support group of colleagues—individuals whom you can go to with questions, individuals with experience whom you can observe and learn from.

4) take responsibility for your own learning—read, take a course, ask for direction, make appointments to meet people who you think might be of assistance to you.

5) reflect on your experience in practice and become self-conscious about what you do and why you do it—that is, develop your personal philosophy of adult education and see yourself as a researcher of your own practice. Because of the contextual nature of program development, the route to effective practice is to reflect on and learn from your experiences—whether you call it good judgment (Cervero, 1989), craft knowledge (Kowalski, 1988), practical knowledge, critical reflection, or something else, this is the key to becoming an effective continuing educator.

"Because educators' practice is rooted in particular sets of circumstances, it is inappropriate to judge their efforts against some fixed ideal of good practice. To know whether practice is effective, it must be judged by what is best in a given set of circumstances. Excellent practice cannot be characterized by a discrete set of knowledge or skills but rather by an understanding of why educators do what they do. At the root of practice are not measurable techniques, but judgment" (Cervero, 1989, p. 111).

I feel that there are a lot of things that you have to develop for yourself—through doing. Although it is really important to talk about program planning and evaluation and all of the developmental stuff, this is something that you have to work through on your own (Ronnie).

Suggested Readings

PROGRAM DEVELOPMENT

Boone, E. J. *Developing Programs in Adult Education.* Englewood Cliffs, NJ: Prentice-Hall, 1985.

Kowalski, T. J. *The Organization and Planning of Adult Education.* Albany, NY: State University of New York Press, 1988.

Lund, B., and S. McGechaen. *CE Programmer's Manual.* Victoria, BC: Ministry of Education, 1981.

Don't panic! When you are feeling overwhelmed, realize that we were all there once. . . . If you are feeling overwhelmed, talk to someone about your feelings. Don't be afraid to ask questions or to ask for help (Blair).

Ask questions and don't be afraid to share your feelings about what you would like to do because that is how you get feedback about whether or not there are problems with doing something or whether you should run with it (Francis).

Sork, T. J., and R. S. Caffarella. "Planning Programs for Adults." In *Handbook of Adult and Continuing Education*, edited by S. B. Merriam and P. M. Cunningham, 233–45. San Francisco: Jossey-Bass, 1989.

Chapter VI

Elements in Program Development

This chapter uses the Sork and Caffarella (1989) model, introduced in the last section, to discuss each of the major components of the program development process. The model is outlined as follows:

- analyze the planning context and the client system

- assess needs

- develop program objectives

- formulate instructional plan

- formulate administrative plan

- design a program evaluation plan.

Although the model is presented in a planning framework, the concept of program development includes both the planning and managing of programs. Development should be viewed as an interactive and cyclical process rather than as one that is linear and finite.

This section is a "must read" if program development still seems more abstract than concrete, and you fear that this manual may never tell you what continuing educators *really* do during their working hours.

Analyzing the Planning Context and the Client System

The Planning Context

The importance of contextual variables in shaping the program development process is discussed in the previous chapter.[1] Two major categories of contextual variables are environmental variables and organizational variables.

Environmental variables include a range of factors that are external to the university but that, nonetheless, create opportunities for or place limitations on the activities of program developers. Some of these variables, like general economic conditions or changing demographic patterns, are beyond the control of the continuing educator. Other environmental factors, like the attitudes of policy makers toward continuing education, may be affected by our actions. Environmental variables can be difficult to identify and, once identified, difficult to understand in terms of their implications for our decision making. For example, will a downturn in the economy make a proposed tuition fee increase unacceptable to adult learners?

The term given to activities directed at gathering information about the environment is *environmental scanning*. Sometimes environmental scanning will suggest a clear direction for action. More often, it provides general support for decision making, or it suggests potential problems and opportunities that the continuing educator can take into account when considering possible outcome scenarios and alternative courses of action.

Environmental scanning is an important aspect of planning new programs. It can help to identify innovative ideas for programming as well as to establish the nature of the "climate" for an idea that is already taking shape. It is also of significant use in program management. Since programs tend to have life cycles, environmental scanning is useful in identifying factors that may effect life-cycle changes. Environmental scanning can identify shifts in attitudes or demographics that may stimulate new interest in a program or suggest that a program is about to enter a period of decline.

---

[1] See Chapter V, p. 81.

I like to think of all of the components [of program development] as being interconnected. There is a relationship among all of them and they are all important. . . . If you only look at one component, you might think that you are making a good decision but, if you don't consider the other aspects, you may not be (Gerry).

[New continuing educators] should understand the educational system of the province in which they are operating. It is important that they get some sense of the ministry and how it works and the internal senior mechanisms of government at the educational level (Dale).

I had a lot of touching base to do with a lot of people to find out how things worked and I fell flat on my face two or three times because I didn't follow the right lines. . . . I really found myself coming back time and again, in thinking about practice, to the importance of knowing your unit, the policies that govern things, the institutional structures within which you work, the kinds of constraints that those put on you, because, if you don't know your environment, you can't work effectively. . . . If you are in a place that supports adult education, you are fighting the institution in quite a different way than if you work in an place that doesn't support adult education (Francis).

The range of environmental scanning goes from highly formalized approaches, such as commercial newspaper clipping services that clip references to topics of interest, to very informal approaches, like keeping notes of conversations with people outside the university context.

There are two typical ways that continuing educators engage in ongoing environmental scanning.

1. Networking—getting involved in community groups, organizations, and associations that are, in some way, relevant to continuing education activities.

2. Trend analysis—reading various newspapers, the literature in a content area, calendars from other CEUs, industry surveys and trend reports, census data, futures literature, and so on.

Organizational variables, such as the extent to which the mission of the university supports continuing education, impact significantly on decision making in program development. For a discussion of key organizational variables and some strategies that continuing educators use to identify and, where possible, manage these variables, refer also to chapters III and V.

The Client System

Sork and Caffarella (1989, p. 237) distinguish between understanding the client system, that is, gathering information about all of those "who are eligible for the attention of the program planner," and assessing needs. In practice, this may not be a distinction that the continuing educator makes. The process of gathering demographic and other general information about those who fall within the boundaries of our attention often focuses, simultaneously, on gathering information to assess educational needs.

The value of the distinction drawn by Sork and Caffarella rests with its implication that needs assessment uses an incremental approach. The first step is to identify the general audience of adult learners that we are interested in and to gather, in a variety of ways, information that allows us to more precisely define this group. If this first "sift" of information does not

I'll tell you frankly that the most useful information that I have gathered in the eight years that I have been involved in continuing education is through my association on the CAUCE Executive. . . . I think my contacts with people across Canada have been extremely useful for me because I have been able to bounce ideas off those people, not only within the Executive but with people at other institutions. And I have been able to get some good ideas from them (Chris).

I suspect that networking might actually be one of the most critical things [that I do]. That is the way that you get your eyes and ears out there in the community as to what's necessary. It is the way that you get your eyes and ears out there in terms of finding the instructors that you are looking for. . . . There are a whole series of networks—professional networks that you are trying to market to, instructional networks, expertise networks, internal administrative networks—and you would be surprised at how they interconnect once you start to get them going (Stacey).

And the calendars of other institutions. I use those a lot for thoughts about how did they deal with this problem or how did they deal with that (Francis).

Although we say on the one hand we are flexible and open, it is really within a particular framework and you have to always pay attention to that. It is not totally open and totally flexible because you can't go doing something that steps on somebody's toes. You've got to be clear about the lines of responsibility and authority (Gerry).

uncover data that deter us, we can proceed to more detailed, resource-consuming methods of needs assessment.

The information that we collect at this first stage will depend on the planning situation, but typically we are interested in knowing:

- How large is this group of learners?

- What do we know about their demographics—educational background, lifestyle, language ability, and whatever else seems relevant?

- What do we know about their general interests, attitudes toward formal education, preferences for different educational formats?

- How can we "reach" this group of learners—is it possible to identify these adults for the purposes of promotion?

The following section on assessing needs describes information sources and approaches that are useful in obtaining the kinds of information described above as well as more specific information on educational needs.

Assessing Needs

Brookfield (1986) talks about the "theory-practice disjunction" in program development; that is, the discrepancy between what is prescribed by models of program development and what actually happens in practice. Nowhere does this discrepancy appear more evident than in the area of needs assessment (Kowalski, 1988).

Although the importance of needs assessment to adult education is generally undisputed, the concept of need has generated considerable disagreement and confusion in the literature (Brackhaus, 1984). The following terms, each with its own nuances, can be found in the writings of adult education theorists: felt needs, real needs, ascribed needs, core needs, created needs, wants, normative needs, educational needs, social needs, organizational needs (Kowalski, 1988). By contrast, adult education practitioners seem much less confused and concerned about the meaning of need. For most practitioners, a need implies a discrepancy or gap between a desired condition or state of affairs and the actual or perceived condition or state of affairs. Educational programs are designed to close or narrow the gap between what is and what is desired.

As Brookfield (1986) points out, the important question, and one that may not get sufficient critical attention in program development, is whose needs are programs designed to meet? Brookfield distinguishes between the felt needs of learners—clearly important to humanistic and democratic approaches and most often attended to in program development—and prescribed needs. Prescribed needs may be based on gaps or discrepancies identified by the continuing educator or by some other group external to the learners (e.g., employers, licensing bodies, advisory groups, the parent institution).

If practitioners are not as perplexed by the concept of need as are theorists, neither are they inclined to adopt many of the formal techniques and procedures described in the program development literature (Kowalski, 1988). Practitioners tend to shun formal needs assessment procedures, like survey instruments and structured interviews, opting instead for informal, exploratory, and intuitive procedures. Some of the reasons for this situation include:

1. Formal needs assessment procedures tend to be expensive and time consuming.

2. They often require knowledge and skills, in areas like questionnaire design and statistical analysis, that practitioners do not have.

3. In many cases, the quality of the information gained from formal procedures is not perceived to be significantly better than that obtained through informal and intuitive methods.

Needs Assessment Methods

The method and scope of a needs assessment depends on the nature of the adult education activity that is being planned. One common way of assessing the need for a short course or seminar

I guess one of the most time-consuming things that I do is when I'm out talking to groups or meeting with people who want a program and I have to work with them around helping them determine what it is that they need. . . . [Sometimes] they just want training but they don't know what that is, so I have to help them discover what that is. And I have to remember where they are and what they are working with and, if I don't know that field as well as I need to, then I've got to talk to people that do. . . . The reality was that the group couldn't afford to develop the program just in their small group, so then it becomes "Who else would be interested?" and at that point it . . . switched from being just negotiating a program with them to developing a collaborative—how many organizations can we draw into this who want the same thing? (Terry)

Needs assessment—we never have any time to deal with that the way that the books say you should do it. We need to have shortcuts. . . . Mostly we fly by the seat of our pants. We do a lot of needs assessment by asking people, on evaluations, what other kinds of courses they want (Blair).

is to base it on potential demand. In other words, for whatever reasons, you have a hunch that a seminar will meet some set of needs. You develop the seminar, hire a resource person, advertise the seminar, and adult learners "vote with their feet." If there is sufficient enrolment to run the seminar, you have met a need.

Adult education activities developed in this way fall on a continuum from those that are "pulled out of thin air"—not a recommended procedure—to those that are based on consideration of informal and secondary needs assessment data—a justifiable approach.

As a general rule of thumb, the depth, scope, and formality of a needs assessment will increase directly with the investment of time and resources required to develop an adult education activity, and with the perceived cost of failure. Comprehensive programs tend to involve a more formal and planned approach to needs assessment than do shorter, stand-alone courses and seminars.

Planning a Needs Assessment

When planning a needs assessment, whether using primary data (i.e., data collected for the specific purpose of the needs assessment) or secondary data (i.e., data collected for some other purpose), or whether using formal or informal approaches, the following points should be kept in mind.

1. Define, as clearly as you can, the purposes of your needs assessment. This will help you to identify the kinds of information that will be most useful in decision making. Avoid collecting information just because it might be interesting. Try to determine how you will use the information that you collect and how it will affect your decision making. Keep it simple.

You think skill "X" is needed out there so you develop a course and you go out and market it and it flies. And the market demand indicates that, indeed, you were right! There was a need for that (Stacey).

2. Define, as much as possible, the scope of the needs assessment and the methods you intend to use to collect information.

   • What kinds of information do you need?

   • Who should be involved?

- What are the existing sources of information?

- If you require information that does not exist and for which you can find no reasonable proxy, how are you going to get the information?

3. Use a variety of methods to obtain information, especially if you are relying on exploratory and informal information sources.

4. Estimate the resources that you will require. Develop a budget and a time frame for the needs assessment. Resource limitations on finances and time are the major reasons why practitioners favour intuitive and informal needs assessment approaches.

Some typical approaches to needs assessment follow. These range from informal and exploratory approaches to more formalized methods of assessment.

1. Secondary sources of data: What can you learn about the needs of adult learners from existing sources of data? Some of these sources will be external to your organization.[2] Other sources will be internal, including, for example, information from registration and application forms, statistics on program participation, the results of program/ course evaluations and previous needs assessments, and telephone requests for program information.

2. Primary sources of data: These range from informal discussions with potential learners or others who have an interest in the program, including employers and content experts, to formal questionnaire designs and structured interviews. Some typical sources of primary needs assessment data include:

- Advisory committees: Since they are composed of representatives from a variety of interested groups, advisory committees can be helpful in identifying needs that can be verified using other data sources. Advisory committees are discussed in more detail later in this chapter.

One important advantage is the computerization of your operation and the access [that provides] to information, tracking information, and [for] comparing. We are in an information era, and having good information on adult participation, completion rates, and so on is important to developing programs. It takes time to build those data bases (Dale).

One of the most important things that I do is to get out to the market to do needs assessment, but time is always a problem. . . . I mean, I go to get the file folder that contains the mail for the day and there are going to be half a dozen little things and, by the time you finish problem solving those half a dozen little things, you discover that it is 2:00 in the afternoon (Jan).

---

[2]   See the discussion earlier in this chapter on environmental scanning and trend analysis.

Advisory committees—they are really your eyes and ears. They provide technical advice in the areas where you don't have the background. They are your sounding board (Stacey).

- Focus group interview: This is an inexpensive, exploratory method that can be used in various stages of program development to generate ideas or to test hypotheses. For additional information on this approach, see the suggested readings at the end of this chapter.

- Questionnaires, structured interviews, and job analyses: All of these methods can be used effectively in needs analysis. They can produce data that are more reliable and valid than the information generated with informal and exploratory techniques, but they are more expensive, time consuming, and require more specialized knowledge for application and analysis. Continuing educators who do not have experience with these approaches, especially with questionnaire design and administration, should consult with researchers who have this expertise.

It takes quite a lot of time to develop advisory committees—identifying people to sit on the committees and then sitting down with them and having the patience to keep working with them. . . . I think one of the most difficult things is trying to assess how much they understand about the issue, how fast you can move along with them, and how fast you can bring them to closure. Lots of times we want to move along faster than the committee is actually ready to. . . . It is identifying and defining the problem, the problem-setting stage, that is one of the most difficult things to do in program development. Once you have done that, things tend to go along a little faster—once the committee is on board and people understand the problem (Gerry).

Working with Advisory Committees

The concept of *collaboration*, or working jointly with others, is a central concept within continuing education. The process of developing programs requires continuing educators to work with learners, with content specialists, and often with representatives of other community groups, such as employers or members of professional associations, who are interested in specific adult education activities. Frequently, advisory committees, which are established by and make recommendations to the CEU, provide the means for ensuring that collaboration occurs.

Based on a national study of CEUs, CAUCE (Brooke and Morris, 1987) reports that most units make use of advisory committees. One of the most important functions of advisory committees is to advise on the various components of program development. Advisory committees may be involved in needs assessment, setting objectives, curriculum decisions, recruitment of instructors, selection of students, program evaluation, and public relations.

Advisory committees are made up of volunteer members who represent various groups interested in, and somehow affected by, the continuing education program. According to the CAUCE survey, typical members include faculty representatives, community leaders, CEU representatives, and part-time adult learners. Members are selected for their knowledge and expertise and for the different perspectives that they bring to the committee. Many of these persons will not be educators; rather, they are individuals who, because of their interests, occupations, or personal experiences, can contribute to the overall process of program development (Kowalski, 1988).

The actual scope of activities of an advisory committee depends on the nature of the program and the practices of the CEU. It is important to realize, however, that whatever its responsibilities, the role of the advisory committee is limited to one of advising and recommending to the CEU. The responsibility for actual decision making rests with the CEU.

In establishing advisory committees to advise on program development, the following points should be kept in mind.

1. Every advisory committee should have terms of reference that outline the purposes of the committee and the responsibilities of committee members, including the expected time commitment, operating procedures for the committee, and terms of office. The size of the committee will depend on a variety of factors, including the committee's responsibilities and the number of community groups it represents, but it should be a manageable size. Probably between eight and twelve individuals is the norm for most advisory committees.

2. The procedures for establishing advisory committees will vary with the CEU. If there are no criteria in place for selecting committee members, these will need to be determined. Criteria usually revolve around issues of:

   - representation—what are the various groups that need to be represented on the advisory committee?

   - knowledge and skills—what knowledge and skills are required of various representatives?

   - commitment—do committee members have the time and the interest to serve on the advisory committee?

3. Advisory committees should be given an orientation as to

There is a lot of work that goes into advisory committees. Getting to a common goal—sometimes that takes a lot of time. People have to see where everybody fits in and they don't always have the same focus. . . . Interestingly enough, it is often the advisory committees that turn out to be the most interesting experiences because of the variety of people and their backgrounds. I've learned about things that I never thought that I would learn about. . . . That part is really quite rewarding—and the commitment of many of the people that we work with, their commitment toward adult education and wanting to do a good job and being involved (Jean).

Perhaps the question you should be asking is what do you really want from the advisory group. What is the purpose of it—and don't be phoney about it. Don't set it up just to say that you have it because you get caught in the end (Toni).

Meeting skills are important—how to plan them, how to conduct them, how to conduct yourself, and how to get the most out of them—because so much of what we do is in that form, whether it is a division or a department committee or whether it be a series of meetings that one holds for gathering information, or advisory committee meetings (Lee).

how the CEU functions, the role of the advisory committee within the CEU, the terms of reference of the advisory committee, and any other information that will assist committee members in carrying out their responsibilities.

4. Much of the work of the advisory committee is conducted within the context of advisory committee meetings and, generally, the CEU member chairs the committee. To ensure that the time of volunteer members is well spent, meetings need to be carefully planned and executed. If you have not had much experience conducting meetings, ask a colleague if you can sit in on his or her next advisory committee meeting.

Planning and Conducting Meetings

The following points may be helpful in planning and conducting advisory committee meetings (or meetings for other purposes).

- Always prepare an agenda. Circulate the agenda and any materials that will be discussed at the meeting in advance. Unless it is unavoidable, do not expect committee members to respond to reports or other documents that they have not received prior to the meeting. The terms of reference for the committee should indicate how much prior notice is normally to be given to members.

- Unless the workload of the committee is very predictable and steady, it is probably advisable to schedule meetings as required rather than on a monthly or bi-monthly basis. Nothing will discourage attendance at meetings more than the sense that time spent at the last meeting was not time well spent.

One piece of advice is to make sure that all the minutes go out on time and that all the members of the advisory committee know what is going on. It's fine to write the minutes but then [you have to] make sure that they've gone out, that people got them, that they got feedback, and they are not feeling left out, and so on (Robin).

- Prior to sending the notice of meeting, make sure that all the administrative arrangements pertaining to the meeting are attended to, and that members are given details about location, start time, and expected duration of the meeting, parking arrangements, and the like.

- Ensure that an adequate meeting facility is booked, room set-up is appropriate, necessary equipment is reserved, coffee or refreshments are ordered, and so on. If you expect clerical staff to attend to take minutes, give them adequate notice.

- Plan the meeting. Decide what you hope to accomplish with each agenda item. If you plan to ask someone to do something at the meeting (e.g., record, lead a subgroup), let them know ahead of time.

- Make agendas doable. Develop a realistic plan as to how long each agenda item will take, including adequate time for participation, and do not plan more activities than the time will allow. As much as possible, try to stay within your time frames. Make sure that meetings start and end on time.

- Members are volunteers and they receive no compensation. Structure meetings and task assignments as democratically as possible. Recognize the participation and the contributions of members.

- Members bring different perspectives, values, and interests to the committee—this is one strength of advisory committees—but it can take time for committee members to understand the process and begin to work as a team.

- Meeting styles can vary in terms of their degree of formality. It is more important that operating procedures are clear to committee members.

- Circulate and approve minutes of every meeting as documentation of the work of the committee. Minutes should be completed and circulated in a timely manner, as close to the meeting date as you can manage.

Working with Partners

Increasingly, the concept of *partnership* is entering the lexicon of continuing educators, although partnerships in various forms have linked adult education providers and community groups for decades.[3] The concept of partnership implies a different kind

---

[3]   See, for example, the discussion of National Farm Radio Forum in Chapter II.

There is the excitement of the advisory committee meeting—but then you have got to come back and write up the minutes. I like it better, or rather I've gotten better at it, because what I try to do is to come back and do them right away. But my tendency would be to wait until next week (Lee).

[The arts program] started up fairly quickly in the sense of coming up with an idea and phoning one of the agencies and saying, "Would you be interested?" and they said, "yes," and then thinking, well, if they are interested, maybe others would be too, and then calling together the group. Well, bringing the group together and trying to develop consensus was a very time-consuming process. We must have gone through six or seven meetings of the five organizations and the university. . . . We were acting as the facilitator. The arts organizations supplied the resources, they supplied the curriculum—so it was sort of a multidimensional partnership. . . . And trying to keep them on track in order to meet our promotion deadlines and whatever was no mean feat, I'll tell you. There were times I wasn't quite sure that this was going to get off the ground, despite the fact that it was a really good idea (Stacey).

How do we measure quality? This is a critical issue for continuing education. Those of us who haven't felt that we have made much progress on access now have to face another pressure and that is . . . don't do anything unless it is very good. Well, if I do very good, then I'll do fewer things. I'll meet fewer people's needs. I'll meet only those people's needs who are in a position to pay for it or [where] somebody else will pick up the tab for it. The resourcing of adult education is, I think, a critical issue. And the importance of finding support and resources, not only from our own budgets . . . but through collaboration. I've been able to do incredible things because people have given their time and energy and effort for free (Robin).

That's where the art of the whole continuing education process is— how do you work with that advisory group or that public or that client group to help them discover what they need and to design the program around that? (Terry)

of relationship between the CEU and community groups than what is found between the CEU and groups represented on advisory committees. Whether the CEU partners with business organizations, professional associations, or community agencies to provide adult education programming, there is generally the implication of ongoing reciprocal rights and responsibilities between the partners.

Partnerships in continuing education can take a myriad of forms, often entailing the sharing of human resources and, sometimes, financial responsibilities. The partnership can be as simple as the donation of equipment to a CEU in exchange for public acknowledgment. Or it can involve something more complex, like collaboration on the development of a new program or the delivery by the CEU of an externally controlled certificate program.

Partnerships are valued because they bring together needed resources for adult education that, individually, the parties involved may find difficult to acquire. Ideally, it is a kind of win-win situation for all the partners where the benefit derived from the partnership is felt to be at least equal to, if not greater than, their contribution.

Some key points about partnerships include:

- Establishing a new partnership may entail a written agreement between the CEU and its partner(s). This task necessitates considerable planning and negotiation and can require legal counsel.

- Partnerships can create potential conflict-of-interest situations for the CEU, or the perception of conflict of interest. Such issues must be examined and resolved in advance of the agreement.

- Roles and responsibilities must be clarified, financial issues decided, and goals and action plans established— to everyone's satisfaction. Procedures for dealing with dissention between the parties must be determined.

- The maintenance of partnership relations will also require a different approach than that needed to maintain advisory committees. In addition to evaluating continuing education programs, there is the need to assess the partnership itself.

Questions to Ask

1. How are needs assessment conducted in your CEU? What kinds of needs assessment data are normally required for program approval? For course and seminar approval?

2. Are advisory committees used in your CEU? If so, for what purposes? Ask someone who works with an advisory committee to provide you with the terms of reference for their committee.

3. What kinds of collaborative/partnership models exist between your unit and other groups internal or external to the university?

Suggested Readings

NEEDS ASSESSMENT

Kops, W. J., and A. Percival. "The Focus Group Interview: A Research Technique for Program Planners." *Canadian Journal of University Continuing Education* 12 (Fall 1990): 31–38.

CONDUCTING MEETINGS

Schindler-Rainman, E., and R. Lippit. *Taking Your Meetings Out of the Doldrums.* San Diego, CA: University Associates, 1975.

PARTNERSHIPS

The Canadian Chamber of Commerce, Focus 2000. *Business-Education Partnerships: Your Planning Process Guide.* Ottawa: The Canadian Chamber of Commerce, 1990.

I guess that I am feeling badly about how I handled this situation. . . . There is this organization . . . and I thought, wouldn't it be interesting for us to collaborate in some way. Well, I guess that I was hoping that they would buy into some of the things that I already had. Well, one should never expect that! Everybody wants something custom made for them and they never have the time to do it. But they suggested a fascinating idea that really caught my attention. . . . They really just wanted me to take it over and to just get on with it and do it. . . . And I have the sense that I have let them down by not responding (Andi).

Developing Program Objectives

Having diagnosed and prioritized the needs of learners and the requirements of the organization, the next task, at least in terms of a logical sequence, is the development of program objectives. A program objective is the anticipated outcome or the result expected from a continuing education program.

There are lots of decisions that we have to make and the books don't tell you how to make them and on what basis you should make them. And lots of times you are making them on the basis of your own intuitive beliefs and values (Gerry).

Programs can have a number of objectives and these can be at different levels. For comprehensive programs, objectives can be broad and general. For example, a general objective for a management certificate program might be "to develop knowledge, skills, and attitudes that are necessary for the development of competent and responsible management professionals." The objectives for specific educational activities within the comprehensive programs are narrower and more precisely focused. For example, for a course in decision making, the objective might be "to be able to illustrate, through written case analysis, an understanding of management decision-making models and techniques and how these are applied in practice."

Knowles (1980) and Boyle (1981) note that objectives can be educational or operational. Educational objectives, like the examples above, focus on what adults are expected to learn as a result of taking part in adult education activities. These objectives will be based on needs and the nature of the subject matter, but they will also reflect our philosophy about how adults learn and our ideas about what constitutes good practice in adult education.

Operational objectives focus on the resources needed to meet educational objectives or on meeting organizational requirements. They can centre, for example, on meeting the administrative needs of the program, such as finding appropriately priced off-campus facilities if this is required.

As part of the planning process, it is important to define anticipated objectives; however, some cautionary words need to be injected into this process.

- It is probably not possible (Apps, 1985) and, according to some, not desirable (Brookfield, 1986) to pre-specify all educational objectives in advance of an educational program. Significant personal learning experiences, including those in which adults come to reinterpret fundamental beliefs and transform their ways of viewing the world, cannot always be predicted or anticipated. Pre-specified objectives should be viewed as open-ended. They are the beginning, and perhaps the core, of what adults are expected to learn, but they do not describe the sum total of what will be learned.

- Adult participants bring their own goals and objectives to learning activities. Instructors need to remain flexible so that they can adapt existing objectives and incorporate new objectives where this seems appropriate. One danger with pre-specified objectives is that instructors may view these rigidly and, especially where no flexible time has been built into the program, feel that they cannot deviate from the pre-set plan.

There may be instances where, because of the extensive knowledge or experience of adult learners, objectives can be written collaboratively between learners and the instructor at the start of the program (Cranton, 1989). In these instances, the instructor enters with broad objectives and these become narrowed and focused in collaboration with learners. In other cases, as with the use of independent learning contracts, educational objectives may be negotiated individually between each learner and the instructor (Knowles, 1975).

• Educational objectives do not have to be stated in terms of measurable behaviours or performance outcomes. Although some types of learning, particularly learning related to psychomotor skills and associated with training, are well suited to performance-based measures, other kinds of learning are not. When educational objectives relate to affective domains of learning—the beliefs, values, motivations, attitudes, and emotions of the individual—it may not be possible to state objectives in terms of performance measures.

Objectives, like other components of the program plan, should be written down. Since instructors may not be involved in the program development process to this point, written objectives are essential in assisting the instructor to develop the instructional plan. Once objectives have been formulated, decisions about content, teaching methods, materials, and evaluation become much easier to formulate.

The first day of a course, we say exactly what participants are going to do and what they are going to try and accomplish—what the objective is. "Are you here for the right reasons?" Because so often I have gotten evaluations back for the course that say the course didn't cover what they thought it would and that's not meeting needs as far as I am concerned (Blair).

Linking Objectives to Success Criteria

Lewis and Dunlop (1991) suggest that, in formulating objectives, program developers need to spend time thinking about

"Approaches to the design of instruction can be placed in a continuum with systematic (some would say mechanistic) approaches at one end and artistic or creative approaches at the other" (Sork and Caffarella, 1989, p. 239).

and discussing their expectations with others who are interested in the program. Related to this, they should identify indicators that they associate with program success/failure and the factors that contribute to success and failure. Once indicators and factors are identified, these can be used to guide planning.

Lewis and Dunlop[4] (pp. 19–22) found that the five most important indicators associated with successful programs are:

- high demand for the program
- participants were satisfied
- increased visibility/credibility/goodwill
- significant participant learning occurred
- high level of participant involvement/interest.

The five most important indicators associated with unsuccessful programs are:

- participants were not satisfied
- planners/instructors were not satisfied
- low/disappointing enrolment
- financial disappointment
- low level of participant involvement/interest.

The five most important factors associated with successful programs are:[5]

- timely/relevant/innovative topic (Assessing Needs)
- effective instructor skills (Working with Instructors)
- good instructional design (Formulating an Instructional Plan)
- good program planning/effective planner (Program Development)

---

[4]   In total, Lewis and Dunlop identify eleven indicators of program success, nine indicators of program failure, twenty-four factors associated with program success, and eighteen factors associated with program failure.

[5]   The bracketed titles refer to sections in the manual that are especially relevant to the success/failure factors.

- good instructional design/content (Formulating an Instructional Plan; Assessing Needs)

The five most important factors associated with unsuccessful programs are:

- poor instructional design/content (Formulating an Instructional Plan; Assessing Needs)

- poor program planning/ineffective planner (Program Development)

- conflicts/lack of institutional support (Understanding the University Context; The Continuing Education Mission)

- ineffective administration/management (Formulating an Administrative/Management Plan)

- inappropriate selection/mix of participants (Assessing Needs; Marketing Adult Education Programs).

Formulating an Instructional Plan

The degree of involvement of the continuing educator in the design of instruction varies. At one end of the continuum, where the continuing educator is also the instructor, or where he or she holds a position in instructional design, the continuing educator will assume responsibility for this component or for major aspects of it. At the other end of the continuum, the continuing educator may be involved in general content and formatting decisions and act as a resource person to the instructor, but the specific content and sequencing of the educational activities are determined by the individual hired to do the instruction.

Two factors that limit the involvement of continuing educators in the instructional design process are lack of expertise in the content area and lack of expertise in principles of instructional design. When advisory committees are used in program development, content experts can be recruited to provide this input, or instructors may be hired to supply the content and the instructional design.

A Path to Building a Curriculum

Determine Evaluation Procedure

Organize Learning Experiences

Select Learning Experiences

Organize Content

Select Content

Formulate Objectives

Diagnose Needs

(Kowalski, 1988, p. 143)

The enjoyment for me comes from working with the group around what it wants and developing the program with them. Then I get the chance to work with instructors, as an instructor or as a co-instructor, and I really enjoy that part. That's sort of the ideal, being involved in instruction, and I know that a lot of [continuing educators] don't get to do that (Terry).

One of the things that strikes me is that a lot of adult education training and sensitization is still predicated upon fairly traditional premises, and that is face-to-face instruction. I think that whole model and paradigm is really falling apart. . . . I think it is important that new practitioners get an appreciation of what I would call the volatility of our field right now and the fact that a lot of our assumptions are breaking down under the impact of technology in education. . . . A lot of the kind of work that we have done in certain fields has now been supplanted by commercially available materials and by public broadcasting and so on. So where we fit in, in terms of where our uniqueness, is something that I think—I hope—that we are beginning to question. We have to look at our own role as adult educators and whether or not the pre-eminence of the formal institution can still be taken for granted. I don't think that it can be (Pat).

Assumptions About Instructional Design

Gagne, Briggs, and Wager (1992) outline five basic assumptions about instructional design.

1. Instructional design is intended to assist individuals to learn and, as such, must consider the diversity of needs, interest and experiences that individuals bring to a educational activity.

2. Instructional design has both immediate and long-range concerns. The focus of the instructional designer can vary from planning a specific learning exercise to integrating learning exercises into topics, topics into courses, or courses into instructional systems for comprehensive programs.

3. Systematically designed instruction can enhance individual human development. It can help to ensure that "no one is 'educationally disadvantaged' and that all students have equal opportunities to use their individual talents to the fullest degree" (p. 5).

4. Instructional design should be conducted by means of a systems approach. The system begins with needs analysis and ends with evaluation that demonstrates the extent to which needs and goals have been met.

5. Designed instruction must be based on knowledge of how human beings learn. This knowledge enables the instructional designer to establish appropriate learning conditions to ensure that the desired effect occurs.

The instructional design process involves the following kinds of activities (Cranton, 1989).

- *Preparing instructional objectives:* Program objectives may be fairly detailed and require little modification, or they may be general and broad and require detailed specification.

- *Selecting and sequencing the content:* This may require the program developer to conduct a task analysis or a procedural analysis to determine the hierarchy of skills or the ordering of steps involved in learning.

- *Designing the instructional process or strategy:* This process involves the selection of instructional methods as well as the teaching materials and the media that are selected.

- *Designing evaluation procedures for the educational activity:* Of concern here is determining whether or not learners achieved the instructional objectives. The methods used will depend upon the nature of the intended learning and can range from formal testing to self-report assessments by learners.

A simple, visual model of instructional design is offered by Rogoff:

THE TRAINING WHEEL *

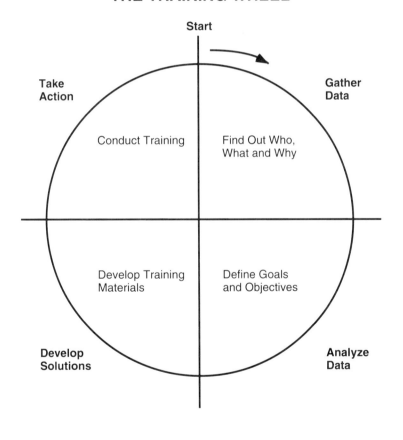

* (Rogoff, 1987, p. 10. Reprinted from the April 1984 issue of *Training*, The Magazine of Human Resources Development. Copyright 1984, Lakewood Publications, Inc., Minneapolis, MN. All rights reserved.)

"Although there is no one set way to order the content, the following general guidelines may be helpful to instructors. First, provide a framework for learners to assist them in organizing their learning. Second, where possible, start with material that may be familiar to the learners so their experience and background can become a part of the learning process. And third, where applicable, integrate practice applications as part of each learning segment" (Sork and Caffarella, 1989, p. 239).

"One debility of using a linear planning model is the tendency to view data in distinct categories. The needs and interests of adult learners, the needs and interests of society, the needs and interests of an organization, and subject matter content often intertwine. Step-by-step methods are more likely to ignore this reality. Rational approaches to curriculum development, much like rational approaches to running organizations (bureaucracy), emphasize objectivity and efficiency. Unfortunately, the real world is filled with barriers that make these goals difficult to achieve" (Kowalski, 1988, p. 144–45).

The approach that we use to develop distance education courses has really developed over the last couple of years. It is a team approach where the instructional designer and the content specialist work as a team and then pull in other resources from around the university. . . . The instructional designer is responsible for the overall course and manages the development process. In addition to acting as a consultant for design issues, such as approaches for the delivery of certain kinds of content or ideas for how student evaluation might be handled, the instructional designer is also responsible for a lot of the administrative and management issues. This allows the content specialist to really focus on the content (Shawn).

"Where distance learning is concerned, life for the instructional designer is assuming a pattern of continuous change, and most of the changes involve the use of technology. Expanded delivery options mean that those articles on appropriate uses of media, formerly read out of curiosity or as a diversion from one's own hidebound system of delivery, become required reading. . . . Technologies for delivery that only recently were out of the question must be reconsidered. And you no longer decide whether to deliver a course by audio cassette, video cassette, print, or audio conference—but *how much, if any, of each* of the options to incorporate" (Calvert, 1989, p. 101).

Instructional Design for Distance Education

Distance education can be defined as "formal instruction delivered mainly to remote locations and/or asynchronously" (Calvert, 1989, p. 93). Although it is often associated with correspondence, other methods such as audio and video conferencing and computer-based instruction, which free the student from regular attendance at the sponsoring institution, are included in the concept of distance education (Thompson, 1986).

The model for distance education in Canada, and for institutions like Tele-université (the University of Quebec), Athabaska University in Alberta, and the Open Learning Agency in British Columbia, is the Open University in Britain which began operation in 1971 (Selman and Dampier, 1991). The Open University took the traditional correspondence approach and embellished it with professionally produced materials, supplementary broadcasts, tutoring and counselling, and residential schools.

Ideally, course development teams that involve faculty members as content specialists, instructional designers, editors, and education technology specialists participate in designing the instructional plan, methods, and materials. Team members participate "as contributing members, not as quasi-clerical assistants" to faculty members (Calvert, 1989, p. 93).

Calvert (p. 94) notes that distance education has several implications for instructional design.

- Traditional classroom instruction provides opportunities for clarifying expectations, correcting misunderstandings and misconceptions, sharing perceptions, and pacing study. Instructional designers must acknowledge these functions and find ways to ensure that these communication needs are met.

- Since distance learners may be far more heterogeneous and form a much larger audience than is the case with traditional instruction, instructional designers must find ways to clearly define the target audience and identify the nature of the diversity that is inherent in the group. The implications of these differences among learners must be considered in the design of instruction.

- Where large audiences are involved, instructional designers must find ways to ensure educational quality while looking for practical strategies for student assessment, feedback, grading,and for handling inquiries from students.

- Student attrition can be a problem in distance education. One issue that instructional designers contend with is that of attempting to sustain motivation through effective instruction.

Educational Technology

An important design consideration in distance education is the selection of instructional media or technologies. Distance educators are advised not to become preoccupied with technology. Instead, they should view technology as a vehicle for delivery while giving primacy to the learner and the message (Garrison, 1987). At the same time, distance educators must have a clear understanding of how various educational technologies will help them to achieve different instructional goals. Blackwood and White (1991, p. 144) identify six principles to guide the selection and implementation of educational technologies.

1. Technologies should be selected with a firm understanding of how they can and should be used.

2. To be effective, the technology must be an integrated instructional component and not an afterthought.

3. Technology should be used to fill identified instructional needs, not just because it is sophisticated and state of the art.

4. Instructors should be involved in making decisions about educational technology.

5. The organization set up to oversee technological resources should see its primary mission as the support of instruction.

6. To be effective, educational technology should be viewed as a means to an end, as opposed to an end in itself.

Some of the technologies that are used in education include print-base electronic technologies (e.g., electronic mail, data-

[Working in distance education] I have to be able to produce materials that are effective for distance learners, to control instructors who want to do things in a way that isn't appropriate for adult students or that isn't appropriate for the mode of delivery, or isn't appropriate given that the students have to use the mail—all of those kinds of things. So, I have to ride herd on all the aspects of course development and delivery (Francis).

One particular frustration is dealing with either departments or professors who are not committed to distance education and who have been coerced in some way into the whole process. . . . Trying to work with individuals who lack this kind of commitment is difficult because then you are not only dealing with the process itself but you have to try and convince the other individual that this is a worthwhile project. . . . But when you can arrange a partnership that really works, both the instructional designer and the content person gain from the experience and it is tremendously satisfying. . . . Content specialists will come back and say that they have learned so much about instruction in general that they have taken their campus courses and entirely restructured them using the kinds of things that they have learned from us during the design process (Shawn).

109

"By the end of the twentieth century, education will have been significantly impacted by the movement of American culture from an agricultural and industrial society to an 'information society.' As a result, contemporary educators will have to devise strategies and implement delivery methods that make information accessible to individuals in the workplace, during leisure, or in the more general pursuit of human potential. To accomplish such a task will require a clear understanding of the nature of information, of the technologies by which information is structured, of the intellectual strategies employed to interpret information, and of the sociocultural milieux created by a technological environment" (Blackwood and White, 1991, p. 135).

base retrieval systems, teletext), electronic teletraining technologies (e.g., teleconferencing, electronic blackboards, slowscan or freeze-frame transmission, full-motion video via satellite or other modes), audio technology (e.g., audio tapes and cassettes), educational video technology, and other data transmission technologies (Blackwood and White, 1991). If you are interested in a review of current educational technologies and their strengths and limitations in achieving different educational purposes, see the suggested readings that follow.

Questions to Ask

1. Are there written program objectives for the programs/courses under your responsibility?

2. If your unit offers distance education programs, what kinds of educational technologies are being used?

Suggested Readings

INSTRUCTIONAL DESIGN

Calvert, J. C. "Instructional Design for Distance Learning." In *Instructional Design: New Alternatives for Effective Education and Training*, edited by K. A. Johnson and L. J. Foa, 92–105. New York: Macmillan, 1989.

Cranton, P. *Planning Instruction for Adult Learners*. Toronto: Wall and Thompson, 1989.

Gagne, R. M.; L. J. Briggs; and W. W. Wager. *Principles of Instructional Design*. 4th ed. Orlando, FL: Harcourt, Brace Jovanovich, 1992.

Rogoff, R. L. *The Training Wheel: A Simple Model for Instructional Design*. New York: Wiley, 1987.

EDUCATIONAL TECHNOLOGY

Blackwood, C. C., and B. A. White. "Technology for Teaching and Learning Improvement." In *Facilitating Adult Learning: A Transactional Process*, edited by M. W. Galbraith, 135–62. Malabar, FL: Robert E. Krieger, 1991.

Garrison, R. "The Role of Technology in Continuing Education." In *Continuing Education in the Year 2000*, edited by R. G. Brockett, 41–53. New Directions for Continuing Education, no. 36. San Francisco: Jossey-Bass, 1987.

Lewis, L. "New Educational Technologies for the Future." In *Handbook of Adult and Continuing Education*, edited by S. B. Merriam and P. M. Cunningham, 613–27. San Francisco: Jossey-Bass, 1989.

Formulating an Administrative/ Management Plan

If there is one thing that continuing educators complain about, it is the administrative requirements of their jobs. Budgeting, marketing, report writing, securing facilities, and numerous other details must be attended to for continuing education programs to function smoothly. There are personnel issues to contend with when dealing with support staff, instructors, and other administrative staff, and disgruntled adult learners to soothe. And managing all of these—the paper and the people— is often the responsibility of the continuing educator.

But if there is almost universal agreement among continuing educators that administrative tasks are tiresome and extremely time consuming,[6] they certainly are not viewed as inconsequential or unimportant. One of the reasons that seemingly well-designed programs fail, or are run as though there is no one at the helm, is insufficient attention to administrative detail. Forgetting to inform students or the instructor about a room change, not having adequate lead time for promotion, or using outdated or inappropriate mailing lists for a direct mail campaign will undermine the best planning efforts.

The way in which CEUs are structured varies and so does the administrative support available to program developers. In some

---

[6] You may recall from Chapter III that continuing educators appear to spend between 29 and 42 percent of their working time on administrative matters.

For every distance course, we have two audio conferences. For each of those audio conferences which run an hour and a half, we have a discussion, using the [teleconference] bridge, with the students at the various centres. We are going to enhance, and we have a video creation station as part of this process, each conference by involving two-way video. The video is going to be created from slides, VCR tapes, transparencies, three-dimensional objects, scanned in photographs, whatever, so that the faculty will then have a video menu that they can call up on the screen . . . and change and modify and, in fact, write on. That will go out to the various centres by way of a phone line. Using monitors, students can respond and ask questions—using either visual or audio means (Dale).

When I start thinking about how I spend my time, I feel a certain amount of frustration. . . . With computer studies, there is so much administration and management required in terms of logistics and facilities planning, making sure the labs are unlocked on Saturdays— just a simple thing like that but, if it goes wrong, all hell breaks loose. And while it seems so simple and easy to do, my secretary usually sends three or four FAXes and I still wonder if I will get a call on Saturday morning—as I have for the past five Saturdays. . . . I don't have an administrative assistant that I can delegate these things to (Andi).

I end up doing a lot of "administeria," which I could well live without but, largely because of budget cutbacks, I'm stuck with. And that is the downside of my job—handling all the detail, and it is the stuff I least like doing and do least well. But it has to be done (Francis).

The administrative details are important but I would just as soon not have to do all of those things. I wish that I could have somebody working closely enough with me that they could take over some of those things because they really bog me down (Jean).

I had some problems this year getting my program schedule set. . . . [An instructor] had committed to me in principle but I didn't have the dates set. I just assumed that she understood how important it would be for me to get that schedule finalized by the end of August. But she didn't call and I kept trying to call her and I got no answer. When I finally did get her in September, she said, "Oh, I saw your letter but I went away for a little vacation." . . . So I've made some notes to myself like, "Next year, when you do the schedule, remember to give instructors deadlines—here is what I am proposing, this is what we discussed, I require this information by this date" (Les).

units, program administration is handled by the same individual who is responsible for all of the planning. In other units, these tasks are shared by program developers and program assistants/managers.

Developing Administrative Schedules and Checklists

One strategy that continuing educators find useful in managing some of their administrative responsibilities is to develop an administrative checklist of things to do, complete with time lines.

To create a checklist and schedule, consider the following approach.

- Identify all the tasks that must be done to accomplish an activity. Begin with general tasks and then break these down into subtasks.

- Working backward from the date of the activity, decide when individual tasks must be completed. Knowing roughly how long each task will take allows you to plan a start date for that task. Be realistic in planning your time lines.

- Where tasks are to be assigned to someone else, build their time requirements into your plan and decide when follow-ups and prompts are in order.

- Put your checklist into a format that works for you—a separate notebook, your appointment diary, a wall or desk calendar. A sample format follows.

TASK SCHEDULE	JAN	FEB	MAR	APR...
1. Develop Proposal for Certificate Review Committee				
2. Meet with Dept Head to Discuss Proposed Changes				
3. Submit Report to Committee Chair				
4. Edit Course Descriptions				

The horizontal lines indicate when the task must be completed. Vertical lines divide the month into two parts denoting the 15th and the 30th of the month (Nilson, 1989, p. 108).

Using this approach, you can develop a planning/management cycle for each program or activity that is under your responsibility—and you can make your checklist as general or as detailed as you feel is necessary. Initially, your checklists will probably be fairly detailed, but as you become more familiar with the planning cycle and your specific responsibilities, you may find that your checklists contain only general tasks and prompts.

As an example, consider the following tasks and time lines for an ongoing certificate program that commences every September. Each task, as illustrated, can be subdivided into subtasks and scheduled into the month. The detailed scheduling of subtasks would be done close to the time that the activity is to begin.

Prior
January: If substantive changes are planned to courses in the program, notify Chair of certificate review committee and prepare necessary paperwork for committee and for Division Council.

Subtasks:

January 2	Write letter to Chair with notification that proposal will come forward February 15 requesting change to the title and content of one course in the program.
January 2	Write proposal—allow three hours to review recommendations of advisory committee and to draft proposal. Submit proposal for typing.
January 11	Send proposal to advisory committee members requesting a response by January 30. Send proposal to department head and arrange meeting to discuss proposed changes with head.
January 17	Meet with department head.
January 30	Call advisory committee members who have not responded to proposal.

I have an administrative assistant who is full time. She is superb in terms of her attention to detail, which allows me to look a lot at the bigger picture, which I really like to do, and manage all the components of what is going on (Les).

One finds oneself spending more time on minutiae than one would like. There are days when I feel very frustrated because I am beseiged with small problems that seem to have to be brought to my attention and I don't accomplish what my own agenda was for the day. I find that very frustrating. I think that you have to be really careful or you can just be swallowed up by those things (Morgan).

I would recommend that [new continuing educators] keep accurate records of what they do—keep a log if necessary and keep notes as to what they do. It makes planning much easier (Shawn).

There is a lot of good information out there in the management literature that is useful to a programmer. . . . I am an educator but I am using management skills and, although my title is not a manager title, that is definitely what I am doing, managing programs (Les).

I spend a lot of time double checking—double checking absolutely everything (Blair).

The fuss of making things through a bureaucracy can be pretty overwhelming. Can you imagine how much simpler our work would be if we had the ideas, worked with people, and then, instead of going through six or seven major channels to make these things happen, just did them ourselves? I'll give you an example—you order audio-visual [equipment]. It may or may not be delivered. Why? Maybe the message didn't get there on time, it got lost, somebody didn't follow up, somebody didn't check it, and yet you are stymied because an administrative detail suddenly takes on enormous proportions. But I see it as unavoidable. It's like the weather (Robin).

I don't know about you guys but we are terrible record keepers. The records are unbelievably awful. So, if somebody walks into this office and says, "OK, I've got this job. Now how do I do it? I'll figure it out from the files." Good luck cause they ain't there. . . . I was absolutely aghast when I came here. I felt like I was some kind of bureaucratic monster. "We want complete files. Document everything!"—which is not really what I am all about but there has to be something left for somebody to pick up the pieces (Stacey).

February:	Submit final proposal to certificate review committee. Review and edit all course descriptions and administrative details for catalogue and certificate brochure and submit revisions to publicist by February 15 (catalogues to be mailed May 15). Review direct mail strategy and existing mailing lists and determine brochure quantities.
	As for January, for each of the several tasks to be accomplished in February, a list of subtasks can be generated and scheduled during the month. Two subtasks related to February have been identified.
Subtasks:	

February 3	Review advisory committee responses, amend draft proposal and resubmit for typing.
February 15	Submit proposal to Chair of certificate review committee.

March:	Review expense budgets for courses in certificate program that ran in previous calendar year. Prepare budgets for courses commencing in September and January and submit to department head by March 20.
April:	Review instructor evaluations and make decisions about instructor reappointments. Contact potential instructors and follow up with a letter of confirmation. Confirm textbooks by May 1.
May:	Plan instructor development workshops for fall. Develop and mail workshop promotion material by June 1.
June:	Send out instructor appointment letters and instructor guidelines for preparation and submission of course outlines, hand-out materials, etc. Prepare copy for August newspaper ad. Submit to publicist by June 15.
July:	For July and subsequent months of the year, continue as above, identifying all the major tasks involved in planning and managing the activity under consideration.

Remember that checklists are planning/management tools to help you stay organized and on time, but they are only as good as the information that informs them. Good planning requires that you understand all the procedures involved in completing a task—who is responsible for what, the paper work that is required, the information that is needed, the time involved, and so on. The first time that you develop a checklist, sit down with a colleague who is familiar with the administrative tasks and talk your way through each task and through the program cycle.

Keep accurate records of your activities so that, if necessary, you can adjust your checklist and improve your ability to plan and manage throughout the program cycle.

Of course, many administrative matters that require the attention of the continuing educator can never be captured by any plan or checklist: a student wants program information, an instructor wants a room change, someone would like to speak to you about teaching opportunities in continuing education. You cannot schedule these kinds of administrative tasks but they are ongoing and they will require your time. One thing that may help is to use your planning cycle to ensure that you do not overbook your time when administrative demands are likely to be greatest. If late August and early September are busy with program advisement, don't schedule meetings during this period unless absolutely necessary. Also, avoid overscheduling your day—any day. Because of the nature of the work in continuing education, you need to plan flexible time into your schedule.

If you feel that you are not well organized—that you spend too much time looking for information that is "right here," that you have problems completing tasks on time, or that important details that should not be forgotten are—consider taking a seminar or reading something on time management. There are lots of different ways to organize yourself and your work, and if this does not come naturally to you, learning about principles of time management is a good investment of your time.

Working with Instructors

Whether or not continuing educators have expertise in instructional design or in the subject matter of the program they are developing, they are often responsible for hiring, orienting, supervising, and assessing part-time instructional staff. Each of these responsibilities is discussed below.

The things that take most of my time are the things that I'll call administrative activities. Some of those include student inquiries . . . approving new students into programs, requests for special consideration on admission, requests for exemptions and transfers. They require looking at, passing on, getting back, and initiating a letter, signing a letter, and that kind of thing. It is a fairly involved process and there are a reasonable number of them. . . . There is also dealing with instructors and their particular needs. . . . An instructor gets a room that is not to his liking. One of the other instructors in the same program got the room that he used to have—and wants. There is not a lot of time spent but there [are] a number of conversations with a number of people to try and make everyone happy. Another instructor calls to see whether he has done about right in terms of how things are graded and where he cuts the students off on marks and so on. There is an enormous amount of time spent on things like that (Lee).

Focusing on the student and working with the advisory committee or the instructor can be at odds. . . . Sometimes you'll have an instructor who says, "Well the students just don't want to work. I have to do it this way. They have to have a final exam." And you have to deal with these attitudes (Jean).

115

Identifying and Hiring Instructors

One piece of advice that I would offer is to hire the very best instructors that you can because they are the ones who represent you in the classroom. My students don't know me, maybe they have never been to [this CEU], they don't really know much about our operation—but the person at the front of the room, that is their teacher and that is how they experience [this CEU] (Andi).

Recruiting effective instructors begins with a clear picture of the kind of person that is required for the program. This will be affected by:

- the continuing educator's theories about adult learning and effective facilitation

- the nature of the subject matter and the kinds of instructional methods that will be used

- the characteristics of potential adult participants.

It is useful to write down job specifications or a job description for the position that includes:

- what the instructor is expected to do in the class (program objectives, instructional methodologies, relationship to students), as well as the instructor's administrative responsibilities

- the qualifications and characteristics of the instructor (these will include academic and/or experiential qualifications as well as personal characteristics that are important to the position, such as flexibility, adaptability, and an understanding of adult learners).

Finding qualified instructors, especially when they are recruited from outside the institution, can be difficult and time consuming. Most continuing educators who have this responsibility are always on the lookout for potential teachers to add to their instructional pool. Some common sources for instructor "leads" include advisory committee members, other instructors, faculty members, and community and industry leaders. Having well-developed external contacts and networks can pay dividends, especially if lead times are short or if the qualifications required by the instructor are highly specialized.

One year I was hiring a whole slew of [computer] instructors and I had a professional development day. . . . At the end, everyone gave a five-minute presentation and . . . you could really tell who was going to be good and who wasn't. . . . My colleagues in private settings do exactly the same thing. They would never think of hiring somebody without a try-out (Andi).

All potential instructors should submit resumes and the names of references who can speak to their qualifications and abilities. The timely acknowledgement of applications and notification of selection decisions will be appreciated by applicants. If suitable positions are not available, the resumes of promising applicants can be kept on file for future consideration.

The Selection Interview

The selection interview is an important method for assessing potential instructors (or anyone that the continuing educator is in a position to hire). If there is no search committee procedure in place, the continuing educator should ask at least one other individual, a colleague from the CEU or a member of the advisory committee, to participate in the interview. The human resources/personnel department within your university can provide you with published guidelines for developing appropriate and legally acceptable questions.

The following "do's" should be kept in mind when conducting selection interviews.

- Conduct the interview in a private setting and ensure that the interview will not be interrupted.

- Create a comfortable atmosphere; begin with general conversation that is unrelated to the interview.

- Prepare interview questions in advance using job specifications as guides.

- Ask "behaviour description" questions; since past behaviour is the best predictor of future behaviour, phrase questions in terms of the interviewee's past behaviour:

  - "Tell me about a time where you experienced conflict with a student. Describe what happened and how you handled the situation."

  - "Tell me about your experiences teaching 'Course X' in the adult education program in the high school."

  - "Describe an experience that you have had that demonstrates effective teaching."

- Listen (easier said than done) and, if necessary, prompt for information.

- Take notes during or immediately following the interview; you may want to rate the interviewee (on a five-point scale) on each of the qualifications and abilities listed as job specifications.

Contact all references and, once your decision is made, contact the interviewee, by telephone if you like, but also in writing.

The instructor orientation Don planned was friendly, informal, and there was nothing authoritarian about it. It was like, "I'm Don [last name]. Call me Don." He tried to make people feel comfortable. He gave them plenty of opportunity to ask questions. You wouldn't even have known that he planned it because it went so smoothly (Les).

Orienting and Developing Instructors

A good orientation that clearly sets out expectations for the instructor and that informs him or her about policies and procedures can circumvent many potential problems. An orientation should outline:

- the mission of the CEU and an overview of other programs and activities of the unit

- academic and administrative policies and rules (ideally, there should be a handbook for the new instructor that outlines everything from grading, exemption, appeal, and payroll policies and procedures, to photocopying and typing requirements, obtaining audio-visual equipment, making room changes, what to do in the event of illness, and so on)

- program objectives and some idea of how the instructor's course "fits in" (one idea, in a multicourse program, is to give each instructor a course outline for every other course in the program)

- a profile of students in the program

- a "Who's Who" that outlines the job responsibilities and phone numbers of everyone in the CEU with whom the instructor will have contact.

If the course has been offered before, new instructors will appreciate seeing previous course outlines and examinations.

Orientations can be done one-on-one with an instructor or with a group of instructors. If individual orientations are conducted, make arrangements for new instructors to talk to former or current instructors teaching in the same program. New instructors will value this opportunity even if their contact is limited to telephone conversations.

If your CEU offers any instructor development workshops or activities, make a special effort to encourage instructors to participate. Whether or not there is an instructor development program, there are several good teaching references available for instructors of adults.[7] Have a few copies of a good teaching reference available to lend to new instructors.

---

[7]   See the Suggested Readings listed under Adult Education Instruction, Chapter V.

Supervising and Monitoring Instructors

Continuing educators are responsible for supervising and monitoring the performance of the instructors that they hire. Although they may have no responsibility for hiring, at times continuing educators are placed in supervisory-like roles in that they have overall responsibility for courses or programs in which instructors are involved. In both cases, most supervision will take the form of helping, and the continuing educator's role will be to serve as a resource person and a problem solver for the instructor.

Where appropriate, sitting in on a class (more as an observer than an evaluator) and using this experience to provide feedback to the instructor is one approach that can be helpful to the instructor. It also gives the continuing educator some insight into the perspective of the adult learner. Unfortunately, when a continuing educator is responsible for numerous instructors or when dealing with distance instruction, attending classes is not a practical approach.

There are other approaches to supervision.

- Suggest that the instructor obtain feedback from students by administering a mid-course evaluation.[8]

- Initiate contact with the instructor on a regular basis; this is proactive, supportive, and should be done even if you think that everything is going well.

- Provide feedback to the instructor on reactions that you receive from adult participants. If participants have concerns related to instruction, they should be encouraged to discuss these directly with the instructor. Unless there is good reason, avoid becoming involved in a dispute between an instructor and a participant until the instructor has had an opportunity to deal with the matter.

- Conduct, without exception, end-of-course evaluations of instructors and provide this feedback to instructors.

Look for ways to recognize and acknowledge your instructors. You may have little to do with setting pay scales but there are other ways that you can reward their efforts.

One thing that I really admire about [this person] is that, as a programmer, she does not feel that she owns the show and that everything has to be hers. She really trusts people. . . . And that is how I try to approach instructors. I trust you as an instructor to make decisions. But there is a difference between that and abdicating your responsibilities. I'm not describing abdicating your responsibilities. I'm describing the knowledge that it takes more than one person to make the program work and that to get the best out of people, you need to give them that kind of trust (Les).

---

[8]   See the Appendix for a sample of a mid-course evaluation.

- Invite them to participate in computer or other seminars that are undersold (the incremental costs of putting your instructors in otherwise empty seats is low).

- Offer a teaching award.

- Provide a framed "certificate of service" to instructors who have taught part-time for five years or more.

- Use your imagination!

Evaluating Instructors and Providing Feedback

Of course, evaluation and feedback are ongoing efforts, and in supervising and monitoring your instructors, you have been assessing their effectiveness and providing feedback and direction.

End-of-course instructor/course evaluations,[9] sometimes referred to as "happiness surveys," provide feedback from students about instructor performance and the value of courses to students. These tend to be most useful in confirming performance extremes—and what, in all likelihood, the continuing educator already knows from telephone calls from participants or others who have inside information. When participants are extremely satisfied or extremely dissatisfied with instruction, end-of-course evaluations tend to reflect this.

Very often, and especially when rating scales and measures of central tendency (like averages) are used, end-of-course evaluations fail to provide much usable information. This situation can be improved if open-ended questions are included on the evaluation. Open-ended questions like "Describe a significant learning experience that you had in this course?" allow participants to make suggestions and to express, in their own terms, their perceptions about the value of the learning.

A good time to share the feedback from an end-of-course evaluation with an instructor is at a "post-mortem" meeting. This provides the instructor with an opportunity to give you feedback about his or her perceptions of the course, the students, and the administration of the course/program.

---

[9]   For an example of an end-of-course instructor/course evaluation, see the Appendix. See also the discussion on summative evaluation in "A Model for Program Evaluation," found later in this chapter.

Dealing with Instructor Performance Problems

Dealing with performance problems is never easy. Once it is clear that there is a performance problem, the role of the continuing educator is to provide constructive feedback and ideas to improve the teaching-learning transaction. Being an effective helping agent requires a grab-bag of knowledge and skills.

> Understanding theories of and acquiring proficiency in human relations, organization, communications, power, influence, leadership, and teaching underlie the power of the helping relationship (Brumfield and Nesbit, 1979, p. 40).

Experience in dealing with performance problems will help you to develop skills in this area. If you encounter a particularly sticky problem or situation, discuss the situation with the person who supervises you.

Effective feedback, which is intended to improve performance, has the following characteristics.

- It is based on an understanding of all the "realities" of a situation; it requires thorough understanding of the problem from the perspectives of those involved.

- It is specific and constructive; it identifies specific performance problems and suggests actual ways of addressing problems. Telling instructors that students are "unhappy" and that they should "try harder" or "work at it" is not effective feedback.

- It is timely; problems are dealt with as they arise. They are not avoided or ignored in the hope that they will disappear.

- It is balanced; as seems appropriate to the situation, feedback should include positive as well as negative elements.

- It is encouraging; again, as seems appropriate to the situation, feedback should convey the sense that the continuing educator believes that the teaching-learning transaction can be improved.

- It is well documented.

Another thing that is difficult is if you have an instructor and the feedback is bad, and the evidence keeps mounting, and then you've got to talk to them about it. That is one of the really tricky, tacky things that you have got to do—to sit down with that person. I'm not very good at that. You skirt around the issue. You mail them the evaluation results. You don't know how to deal with it up front (Gerry).

Developing Educational Budgets

As a component of administrative planning and management, budgeting is integral to program development. It should not be viewed as something separate or apart from program development.

An educational budget is a planning and management tool. It can be defined as "the numerical translation of educational programs into a strategy of expenditure and revenue that supports the overall educational plans" (Holmberg-Wright, 1982, p. 25). The budget documents the financial plan for the program or educational activity. It identifies the costs or *expenses* that are anticipated for the life of the budget as well as the expected income or *revenue*.

Kowalski conceptualizes the relationship between program planning and budgeting as an equilateral triangle. One side is the expenditure plan, the other side is the revenue plan, and the bottom is the program plan. If one side is reduced, the other sides also must be downsized. For example, if revenues are expected to be lower than initially forecast, expenses must be reduced (or new revenue sources sought). One way to reduce expenses might be to shorten the length of the program.

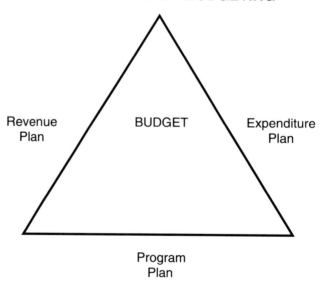

COMPONENTS OF BUDGETING

Revenue Plan — BUDGET — Expenditure Plan

Program Plan

(Kowalski, 1988, p. 164)

Program expenses can be broken down into three basic categories: developmental costs, delivery costs, and evaluation costs. Costs can be further classified as *direct* (or variable costs) and *indirect* (or fixed/overhead costs).

Direct costs are those that are incurred because you decide to run a program. Costs that can be assigned to programs typically include instruction, textbooks or hand-out materials, food, most promotion costs, and facilities rental.

Indirect costs cannot be assigned directly to programs and are generally thought of as operating costs. Typical indirect costs include your salary and the salary of other permanent CEU staff, telephone, lighting, heating, office supplies, and office rental.[10]

Program revenue sources include tuition fees, grant or contract income, or some combination of these. In addition, the CEU may receive a central budgetary allocation from the university which, although it is not program revenue, may influence the amount of revenue that the program is expected to generate. For example, programs may be expected to generate sufficient revenue to cover:

- all direct costs and all indirect costs

- all direct costs and some contribution to indirect costs

- all direct costs but no indirect costs

- some portion of direct costs.

Budgeting procedures, including revenue expectations (i.e., the costs that the educational event is expected to cover), and the way that expenses are coded and assigned vary from CEU to CEU.

Even within a CEU, differences, especially in revenue expectations, can be found between program areas. Given that budgets are tools to help achieve program objectives, these differences are not surprising. Programs that have lower revenue potential, perhaps due to participants' inability to pay, may be assigned lower revenue expectations than programs for which

---

[10]   CEUs often allocate some percentage of indirect costs to individual programs. For example, in some CEUs, salary costs are allocated to programs on the basis of time. If a continuing educator estimates that 10 percent of his or her time is spent on a particular program, 10 percent of his or her salary may be charged against that program.

We have developed a budget system here that allows us to track our costs by mode of delivery, distance or classroom, by term, by location. So when I look at a given location, I can look at direct and indirect costs and the income tracked against that. . . . We know what is making money and what is losing money for us and, when that question gets asked, we can answer it (Dale).

One question that a new person needs to ask is, "Who owns the budget?" I thought that I did and that I was responsible for it, but I finally decided that I didn't own the budget. That is how I coped with the fact that, without telling me, the department charged things to my budget (Les).

I should be giving more attention to budget planning. The reason that this area has not been as important is that we have really lagged behind in terms of our financial management and the software that we have and so on. We just don't have a lot of tools at our disposal for using budgetary information and analyzing it properly. But we are moving in the right direction (Morgan).

Sometimes what you need to do is take a look at what the actual costs were the year before. If they seem about right, up them all by a small percentage [to take care of inflation]. What I learned this year is that a budget is just a plan (Les).

123

The financial administration in my program is pretty complicated. There are special funding arrangements and working out who is going to be invoiced for how much isn't easy. There isn't any direct payment—you have to invoice all these different groups. And then there is the accountability—all the attendance records and grade sheets that have to go to all the sponsors. It's all different. There is no pattern (Terry).

Budgeting—very clear instructions have to be given [to a new continuing educator] about what the expectations of the program area are to meet budget requirements. What are its resources? What are the flexibilities of judgment within those budgets? Can you, for example, borrow from Peter to pay Paul? . . . A budget is an important item. It isn't something that you just write down and put away (Robin).

As soon as I started my job, I was handed monthly statements from the finance department. I didn't have a clue how to read these things and my dean at the time was no help. So I finally just called someone in the finance department and swallowed my pride and said, "Look, I don't know how to read these things. Would you come over and give me a lesson?" (Morgan)

there is strong demand and employer tuition reimbursement.

To develop your expense budget, you need to:

- identify the costs that your program is expected to cover

- obtain realistic estimates of these costs.

To develop your revenue budget, you need to:

- identify all sources of revenue

- project realistic revenue targets (e.g., number of expected participants times the projected tuition fee).

If the projected revenue is not adequate to cover anticipated costs, you can attempt to increase revenue (e.g., increase tuition fees or look for grant money), or you can try to decrease costs (which may involve changing the program plan).

Budgets refer to projections, actuals refer to outcomes, and variances refer to differences between budget and actual (variances can be positive or negative). Ideally, what you budget for expenses and revenues will be very close to your actuals, and the closer the better—this indicates that your planning and forecasting were accurate.

You may hear continuing educators talk about *breakeven*. The breakeven point refers to the number of registrations required to cover the full costs of the educational activity but not generate any surplus. In traditional accounting terms, full costs include all direct and indirect (variable and fixed) costs. For continuing educators, the definition of breakeven is more likely to be based on the costs that the program revenue is expected to cover. Expectations vary between CEUs, so breakeven is a relative concept that will mean different things in different CEUs. Too, unless breakeven refers to all direct and indirect costs, revenue over the breakeven point is surplus, but it is not profit. Profit is generated after all direct and indirect costs have been covered.

A similarly confusing and relative term is that of *cost recovery*. If someone says that their programs are cost recovery, the first question to ask is, "What costs are your programs expected to cover?" Full-cost-recovery programs recover all direct and indirect expenses.

The Appendix contains a sample budget proposal form for nondegree programs.

Marketing Adult Education Programs

Marketing is a management function that is critical to the survival of the CEU.[11] Unfortunately, it is a function that is both poorly understood and poorly executed by many continuing educators. Those who equate marketing with promotion or selling tend to give marketing little thought until most of the planning for an educational activity has been completed. When marketing finally enters the picture, concern tends to focus on designing attractive brochures or on developing catchy mottos for advertising. There is very little planning to achieve program objectives, and the benefits of marketing are not realized.

Simerly and Associates (1989, p. 10) defines marketing as "the overall process of studying, analyzing, and making decisions about how best to serve consumers with continuing education programs and services." Concern is with understanding the needs, values, and attitudes of the adult learner and the sponsoring organization. Once needs are defined, a marketing plan can be developed that addresses these needs, informs adult learners, and motivates participation.

Kotler (1985) sees marketing as an exchange process whereby adult learners, by participating in continuing education, exchange value (e.g., time, money, and lost opportunity) for value (e.g., stimulating learning experiences, sociability, the potential for career advancement, credentials). To Kotler, marketing is not promotion or selling, but the attempt to maximize value to the adult learner to encourage the exchange process.

Both Simerly and Kotler take the position that, while marketing is a management function, its effective practice depends on balancing the needs and interests of adult learners against those of the institution. Unfortunately, the process sounds somewhat simpler than it is, and ethical dilemmas are an inherent aspect of marketing decision making (Burns and Roche, 1988).

Sales conjures up images of your local car dealership or siding salesmen and [programmers] don't want any part of that—they don't see that as part of the university. . . . You get this great instructor, you do all this work, you run some kind of an ad in the newspaper, and then you wait for [participants] to come charging through the door. And when they don't, you say, "But, gee, it was such a good idea." In fact, with a little work [i.e., marketing] you could have turned it around and maybe salvaged something that was, indeed, a good idea (Stacey).

Another piece of advice is to pay attention to external relations because, after all, we are in continuing education and it is externally oriented. It is, and some universities recognize this, a critical public relations arm of the university. [New continuing educators] need to be aware of that dimension and to see programs, not as cash cows, but to see that in the marketing of programs, we are in effect representing and marketing the university (Jan).

"Marketing . . . deals with the many methods by which A tries to get B to do his will, where B has the freedom to act as he chooses" (Rados, 1981, p. 17).

---

[11]   As with program planning, marketing occurs on different levels within the CEU. Macro-level programming involves long-range planning and is often closely tied to the strategic plans of the CEU and to achieving its mission and goals. For example, recognizing the value of adult learners as a resource to the organization will lead to plans to develop a strong customer service orientation and an image of high quality/good value programming. Micro-level marketing deals with an annual planning framework and focuses on achieving specific marketing objectives, often associated with specific educational activities. Comprehensive programs require both macro- and micro-marketing.

The "4 P's" of the Marketing Mix

"Marketing is the analysis, planning, implementation, and control of carefully formulated programs designed to bring about voluntary exchanges of values with target markets to achieve institutional objectives. It involves designing the institution's offerings to meet the target market's needs and desires and, using effective pricing, communication, and distribution to inform, motivate and service the markets" (Kotler and Fox, 1985, p. 7).

You need a good program but you also need to be able to communicate through your brochures and calendars that this is a good program. If you can convince people out there, you have a skill that is very important for a programmer (Chris).

Marketing applies even to the packaging of course materials. We have some instructors who come in with their own overheads—they are typewritten and cramped. We try to upgrade them—big, bold, very few words. . . . And people don't like fourteenth-generation photocopies either (Les).

Simerly's definition of marketing might lead you to think that, in talking about needs assessment, setting objectives, and designing the instructional plan, we have already been talking about marketing-like activities. In fact, developing the program based on the needs of adult learners and the requirements of the organization is one key component in the marketing plan. In other words, if program development follows the kind of process described earlier in this chapter, many of the activities described in this section will already be under way.

There are four components or variables, referred to as the "4 P's," that continuing educators can manipulate in developing a marketing plan.

1. *Product:* The product refers to the sum total of what we have to offer the adult learner. It includes the actual educational activity as well as the services and benefits associated with participation (e.g., information sessions, counselling, library access). This is the most important component in any marketing strategy.

2. *Promotion:* Promotion refers to all of the various ways that we communicate the existence and the benefits of our programs to adult learners. Our efforts are directed at encouraging adult learners to participate in adult education. There are five basic means of promotion, each of which has advantages and disadvantages (Beder, 1986):

   • advertising—includes all forms of paid promotion

   • publicity—includes all forms of unpaid promotion

   • face-to-face communication—includes direct selling as well as word-of-mouth promotion

   • incentives—include tangible items like give-away coffee mugs or pens, as well as intangibles like early registration discounts and late fee penalties

   • atmospherics—the message conveyed to the adult learner through the physical environment and the location where the educational activity is held.

   Direct mail advertising and word-of-mouth promotion appear to be the most effective ways of promoting adult education activities (Smith and Offerman, 1989).

3. *Price:* Once program costs are determined, revenue expectations can be set and a pricing strategy can be selected to set fees for an educational activity. Essentially, there are three pricing options:

   - cost-oriented pricing—enrolments are projected and fees are set to cover projected costs (or costs plus whatever surplus is desired)

   - demand-oriented pricing—fees are based on what the market will bear

   - competitive pricing—fees are set on the basis of what competitive providers are charging for similar educational activities.

4. *Place:* The final variable in the marketing mix is that of location, or where an educational activity is held. While convenience and comfort are tangible aspects of location, there are symbolic meanings associated with location that can influence the decision to participate in adult education. For example, taking a business program in a training facility designed especially for executives conveys a different message to participants than taking the same course in a church basement.

The Marketing Plan

Designing a marketing plan for an educational activity involves designing a *marketing mix.* This mix is a combination of the variables of product, promotion, price, and place that is attractive to a segment of adult learners (i.e., the target market) and that motivates them to participate in adult education.

The concept of market segmentation is critical to the development of a marketing plan. Market segmentation refers to the process of dividing the total, heterogeneous market of adult learners into submarkets or segments, each of which tends to be homogeneous in certain significant respects. Homogeneity may be due to a combination of the following kinds of variables:

   - demographic—such as age, occupation, education, ethnicity, religion, or social class

A major component of my work in program development was basically to communicate that idea, and I did it at several levels. I had to communicate it to [participants], in other words, write the publicity, write the program descriptions, and so on. I had to, at the same time, communicate it to those people who would be in a position to allocate resources to it, writing proposals, writing notes from the advisory committee meetings—just to make sure that people are communicating (Robin).

It is really important for front-line people to create a friendly type of atmosphere. When someone calls, it instills in their minds that, "Gee, this is a friendly type of place." They might not think much about it but that is how they will feel and maybe that will influence their decision to take a course (Sandy).

We went to a lot of trouble to find this place [i.e., a rural hotel to accommodate a residential program]. We wanted the program to reflect a certain level of quality and that entered into every decision that we made. . . . It is not a luxury health spa resort, but it is very comfortable and pleasant and relaxed (Les).

"The aim of marketing is to make selling superfluous. . . . The aim of marketing is to know and understand the customer so well that the product or service fits him and sells itself" (Drucker, 1974, p. 5).

- geographic—urban or rural, area of the city or province

- psychographic—lifestyle, values, interests

- behavioural—level of experience, area of specialization, purchase behaviour.

Failure to segment the market of adult learners means that the components of product, promotion, price, and place cannot be tailored to the needs of any particular group. Undifferentiated or mass marketing, which involves no segmentation and therefore assumes that adult learners are "all the same," generally does a poor job of serving anyone's needs.

Market segments that interest the continuing educator will share three characteristics.

1. They will be substantial—large enough, over the expected life of the program, to justify the marketing effort.

2. They will be measurable—segmentation variables must be subject to some kind of measurement so that you can distinguish those who belong to the segment from those who do not.

3. They will be accessible—to effectively promote a program to a segment of adult learners, you must be able to reach them in some way.

Burns and Roche (1988, p. 57) identify four ingredients in a marketing plan.

1. *A statement of purpose clearly outlining the mission of the organization and the current situation.*

   The first component of program development discussed in this chapter involves the analysis of the planning context and the client system. This process focuses attention on organizational needs and on those segments of adult learners that present program development opportunities to the continuing educator.

We are doing a lot more target marketing, rather than using a generic newspaper ad or a radio ad. They have their place but they are not as effective as a targeted approach (Dale).

2. *A comprehensive identification of the consumer needs that the institution seeks to serve.*

   The techniques used in environmental scanning, as well as methods of needs assessment, generate the information (i.e., *market research*[12]) that enables the continuing educator to identify the needs of the target group with respect to the variables of product, promotion, price, and place.

Of special interest to marketing are questions relating to the kinds of promotion methods that will effectively reach the target group of adult learners, and their reactions to price, location, and formatting issues.

3. *A statement of specific objectives outlining how the resources of the organization can best be utilized to fulfil its mission and meet identified needs.*

As with any type of plan, marketing plans require objectives. Marketing objectives focus on reaching and motivating adult learners. For example, one objective will almost certainly be to obtain a certain number of registrations. A promotion objective might be to increase awareness about the program among members of the target group. Another promotion objective could focus on increasing the amount of support that employers provide through tuition reimbursement (employers may not be part of the target group, *per se,* but they may be one of the "publics"[13] that you will have to consider in developing marketing plans for your group of learners).

Objectives should be designed to enhance the overall goals, tone, and image of the university and the CEU. In fact, projecting a particular kind of organizational image is a central aspect of any marketing plan.

4. *A strategy outlining how the program will be developed, priced, and communicated in light of the stated objectives.*

Having established marketing objectives, a marketing timetable can be developed and cost projections obtained. Decisions must be made regarding program design, a promotion plan, a pricing and a location strategy. Ideally, all of these decisions will interact to maximize value to the

"As in other aspects of adult education, there are no easy answers about what constitutes ethical or unethical [marketing] behavior. The best assurance of ethical practice by adult educators seems to come from an awareness of the various sources of conflict that are inherent in marketing and in the decision-making process" (Burns and Roche, 1988, p. 63).

Whatever [promotion] comes out of this department has to look professional, has to feel professional, and the person who reads that material has to feel wanted and think, "I'm being courted" (Chris).

Sometimes people write brochures before the curriculum has been finalized and that can create real problems. The brochure has to be as accurate and as close as possible to what the participants are actually going to get in the course. To do that properly, you have to have worked out the curriculum in advance (Blair).

---

[12] Market research generally implies a broader focus than does needs assessment. Whereas the latter focuses on the needs of adults with respect to educational programs, the former also focuses on questions related to promotion, place, and price. The author uses these terms interchangeably.

[13] Another important public is the university community. As Chapter III suggests, internal marketing can be as important to a CEU as marketing to external groups.

We track every call and why people call so that we know what works and what doesn't work (Dale).

adult learner—to produce the *right product, in the right place, at the right price, and promoted to the right market.*

Many of these marketing decisions involve as much art (and good judgment) as science, but there are lots of "how to" sources available, especially around the design of promotion—how to design brochures and write copy, how to develop news releases, how to design effective advertising campaigns, how to create effective mailing lists. Since many continuing educators are involved in writing brochure copy, a Brochure Preparation Checklist (Leffel, 1983) is included in the Appendix. For additional information on the how to's of marketing, see the suggested readings that follow at the end of this section.

A final aspect of marketing is, of course, to track results and to find ways to assess the effectiveness of marketing decisions. As Simerly and Associates notes, "The most elaborate marketing plans and expensive advertising pieces are not effective if they do not produce the number of registrants required to break even with respect to the program's financial goals" (1989, p. 450).

To help ensure that marketing decisions are sensitive to inherent conflicts in values and to ethical dilemmas that may arise in marketing, Burns and Roche (1988, p. 61) pose four questions that continuing educators should ask about all of their marketing decisions.

1. Does our proposed action conflict with the purpose or mission of the institution as I understand it?

2. Would the proposed action meet genuine consumer needs in the marketplace, as I understand those needs?

3. Is the action consistent with the objectives we have set forth for the program?

4. Is it feasible for our organization to deliver the program with the resources at our disposal?

Questions to Ask

1. What kinds of instructor orientation/development does your CEU do? Is there an instructor handbook? If you haven't seen copies of mid-course evaluations or end-of-

course instructor and course evaluations, ask for these.

2. How does the budgeting system work in your CEU? Have you seen budget forms? Who approves budgets? What are the budget requirements for programs under your responsibility?

3. Does your program area have a marketing plan? A marketing budget? What promotion methods are used? How are they evaluated?

Suggested Readings

SUPERVISION

Hodgetts, R. M. *Effective Supervision: A Practical Approach.* New York: McGraw-Hill, 1987.

Lussier, R. N. *Supervision: A Skill-Building Approach.* Homewood, IL: Irwin, 1989.

BUDGETING

Shipp, T., ed. *Creative Financing and Budgeting.* New Directions for Continuing Education, no. 16. San Francisco: Jossey-Bass, 1982.

MARKETING ADULT EDUCATION PROGRAMS

Beder, H., ed. *Marketing Continuing Education.* New Directions for Continuing Education, no. 31. San Francisco: Jossey-Bass, 1986.

Simerly, R. G. *Planning and Marketing Conferences and Workshops.* San Francisco: Jossey-Bass, 1990.

Simerly, R. G., and Associates. *Handbook of Marketing for Continuing Education.* San Francisco: Jossey-Bass, 1989.

"... Develop methods to track the results of every marketing project. Track all mailing lists to determine which lists drew the most responses. The lists resulting in telephone and in-person registrations must also be identified.... Registration staff must be trained to make appropriate inquiries during telephone registrations. For example, is the caller responding to a direct-mail brochure or to a newspaper ad? These data must be recorded in a uniform fashion so that they can easily be analyzed" (Simerly and Associates, 1989, p. 450).

Designing a Program Evaluation Plan[14]

Program evaluation—our life depends upon delivering quality. You cannot deliver second best because then you are third rate (Dale).

Evaluation involves making judgments about the value or worth of a program. The emphasis is on generating information that can be used to improve and enhance adult education programs. Through evaluation, continuing educators attempt to increase their understanding about how to create adult education that is valuable and meaningful to participants (Steele, 1989).

Evaluation is a process whereby information is collected to make decisions about continuing education programming. This definition of evaluation highlights some important aspects about the nature of program evaluation.

- As a process, evaluation is an ongoing cycle of activities that continues throughout the life of the program.

- Its purpose is to make decisions related to the program.

- It is based on accurate and considered information.

Formative and Summative Evaluation

Although, in reality, the distinctions can be blurred, evaluations tend to be dichotomized into one of two categories: formative evaluations and summative evaluations (Deshler, 1984). Formative and summative evaluations can be conducted for programs or courses, although the former process tends to be more complex. For example, comprehensive programs, in addition to ongoing instructor/course/fiscal evaluation, usually undergo periodic in-depth and systematic evaluation after completing a specified number of course cycles.

A *formative evaluation* occurs while a program is in progress. Its intent is to make improvements to the program. Formative evaluations are often used by instructors during a course to ensure that instructional objectives are being met. The focus of the evaluation may be on the effectiveness of any of the components of the course (e.g., objectives, sequencing of materials,

"Deciding what to evaluate is a critical part of the evaluation process. A good way to start is to frame the evaluation questions and issues within the context of the program objectives. Adult educators should always be concerned about whether programs produce expected learning results" (Sork and Caffarella, 1989, p. 241).

---

[14] See an earlier discussion in this chapter on instructor evaluation, which is part of the program evaluation process.

learning materials, methods, assignments, grading procedures) and/or on the effectiveness of instruction (e.g., establishing learner expectations, pacing, asking or responding to questions, closure, level of difficulty, effective use of teaching methods, stimulating interest and enthusiasm) (Cranton, 1989, p. 184).

For formative evaluations to be effective, they must be conducted early enough in the program that changes and modifications can be made. There are numerous formal techniques and methods that can be used (Beatty, Benefield, and Linhart, 1991), but often instructors and program developers simply construct a questionnaire that they administer to program participants. An example of a formative mid-course evaluation that is used in management certificate courses in the Continuing Education Division at The University of Manitoba is included in the Appendix.

A *summative evaluation* occurs once the program is complete. It can have many purposes including: to account for program decisions and expenditures; to provide information about how well program objectives were met; to identify ways to improve future offerings of the program; to identify other needs; and to meet the evaluation requirements of sponsoring organizations.

An example of a summative evaluation that is used at the end of each management certificate course in the Continuing Education Division at The University of Manitoba is included in the Appendix. The purpose of this evaluation is to provide one source of evaluation information, in this case from students, about the content of the course, the quality of instruction, and the quality of program administration.

As was noted in the earlier discussion on instructor evaluation, summative evaluations administered at the end of a course are often of limited value. The usefulness of these evaluations, sometimes referred to as "happiness surveys," can be improved by using open-ended questions (in addition to simple rating scales and checklists), by ensuring that participants are given appropriate and adequate time to complete the evaluation, and by conveying to participants the importance of feedback in identifying areas for improvement. Too often, these surveys are squeezed, with little introduction, into the closing moments of a learning activity—an approach that is unlikely to convince participants that evaluation is an important part of the educational process or that their comments, positive and negative, are valued.

A lot of times adult educators are terrible thieves. And I don't think that is bad. What we do is pull things together—so I found two or three little evaluations and I just kind of played around with them until I came up with something that would work with my program. . . . The first three or four questions are scored numerically—high degree of satisfaction to low degree. But the rest of the questions—there are only ten or twelve—are very open-ended. They are things like, "What did I learn at this session that will help me in my job?" So they are not only helpful for me in evaluating how useful the learning experience is, but they also encourage the learner to reflect on what they did and what they learned. . . . I've done evaluations so simply as to just give everybody an index card that says, "I found this program to be . . . ," and ask them to complete the sentence (Les).

133

In some places, if the faculty are not very much involved in program evaluation, they can cause incredibly difficult problems for the program developer (Robin).

A Model for Program Evaluation

A simple model[15] of program evaluation includes the following.

1. *Identify the purposes of the evaluation: decide what to evaluate.*

   While evaluations may begin with questions related to whether or not program objectives were met, they seldom end here. Because there are many stakeholders to any adult education program, and because these people have different interests, evaluations generally have multiple purposes. CEU administrators will be interested in accountability issues. Teachers will be interested in learners' perceptions about the quality of instruction and in learning outcomes. Participants will be interested in understanding how they have done in the program relative to the expectations of the instructor, or relative to other participants. Continuing educators will be particularly interested in the learners' perception of the value of the program and the services received, and whether or not program objectives were achieved.

   At this point, it should be apparent why this manual has devoted so much attention to philosophy and principles of good adult education practice. If these have infused the program development process, evaluation will be concerned with, among its other objectives, the extent to which philosophical purposes and principles of good practice have been met.

2. *Decide on the evaluation design: determine who will be involved in the evaluation, what information needs to be collected, how the information will be collected.*

   In discussing the assumptions of andragogy,[16] Knowles (1980) advises program developers to focus evaluation on adult learners and to involve them in the design, collection, and interpretation of data. While learners certainly must be included in the evaluation process, it is an oversight not to include representation and input from other stakeholders to the program.

---

[15] The cautionary comments about using models in program development, discussed in Chapter V, apply to the use of models in program evaluation.

[16] For a discussion of andragogy, see Chapter IV.

Although procedures vary from CEU to CEU, the design and implementation of a program evaluation will often have input from people who are not instrumental to the program development process. The continuing educator responsible for the program and representatives of the advisory committee may be members of the evaluation team, but the Chair is often a CEU member who is not involved with the program or someone outside the unit. This arrangement attempts to deal with some of the ethical dilemmas inherent in conducting evaluations.

There are a variety of sources and methods that one can use in collecting evaluation data and many of these are also useful in assessing needs—from organizational records on registrations, course and instructor evaluations, and student performance to questionnaires, interviews, focus groups, and other data collection approaches especially designed to collect evaluation data.

Resource limitations, both in time and money, often force those doing evaluations to look for expedient and inexpensive ways to collect data. Under these conditions, multiple approaches to data collection will help to ensure that those conducting the evaluation obtain the best possible understanding of the program's value (Steele, 1989).

3. *Establish evaluation criteria, analyze the data, make decisions or recommendations regarding the program.*

Trying to determine whether or not a program has merit is not as simple as it sounds. Developing measurable criteria for certain objectives, like those relating to participation and to budgetary matters, are reasonably straightforward.

It is much more difficult to establish criteria for less tangible program outcomes, such as the ability of the individual to think critically or to assume greater independence (Sork and Caffarella, 1989). Since these objectives may not be measurable in quantitative terms, qualitative appraisals will be required (Kowalski, 1988). Unless program developers have spent time setting up their objectives and thinking about indicators of success and criteria for evaluation, there is the danger that evaluation will rely too heavily on factors that are easy to measure but contribute little to our understanding of how to improve and

Evaluation is critical but I think that, by and large, universities do not do this very well. They don't have proper output measures. Our output measures are numbers of degrees, or numbers of certificates, or just plain numbers of bodies and I'm not sure that those are the output measures that we should have. For skills training, part of our evaluation should be long term and maybe we should steal a book out of the Fed's manual where Employment and Immigration Canada has thirty-day, sixty-day, and twelve-month follow-ups. They are looking for certain kinds of things like labour force attachment—Did you get a job? Did you have a job a year later? Did you get a job immediately, two months later, twelve months later? ... And particularly in our skills areas, those may be much more important measures for us (Stacey).

"There are many lessons to be learned about successful planning from the ashes of our failures" (Sork, 1991, p. 12).

enhance adult education programming.

Once criteria are established, program strengths and weaknesses can be identified. Since the purpose of evaluation is to make decisions to improve programs, this is the next logical step. In making such decisions, the cycle begins again.

If one important reason for conducting program evaluation is to learn from our experiences so that we can become better program developers, analyzing program failures can be as important as analyzing program successes (Sork, 1991). Analyzing and reflecting on our experiences in practice provides support for our theories of adult education and our understanding of good practice, or it can lead us to rethink our ideas and change our practices.

Kowalski (1988) offers the following model for program evaluation.

A MODEL FOR PROGRAM EVALUATION

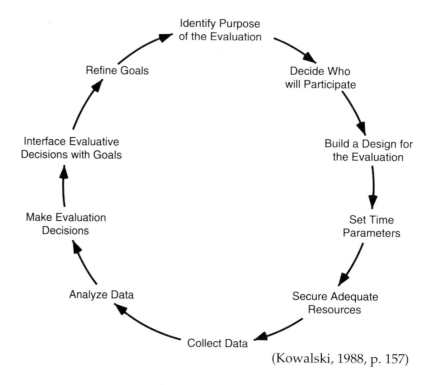

(Kowalski, 1988, p. 157)

In offering this model, Kowalski notes that this is only one alternative to constructing program evaluation. Although it can serve as a guideline, each program evaluation situation is unique. The program evaluation process should be tailored to the specific purposes of the educational activity and to the information needs of stakeholders to the program.

Questions to Ask

1. Identify the program evaluation methods that are used in your CEU. Is there a requirement for systematic program evaluation? Are there any existing evaluation reports for your programs?

Suggested Readings

EVALUATION

Beatty, P. T.; L. L. Benefield; and L. J. Linhart. "Evaluating the Teaching and Learning Process." In *Facilitating Adult Learning: A Transactional Process*, edited by M. W. Galbraith, 163–92. Malabar, FL: Robert E. Krieger, 1991.

Deshler, D., ed. *Evaluation for Program Improvement*. New Directions for Continuing Education, no. 24. San Francisco: Jossey-Bass, 1984.

Patton, M.Q. *Qualitative Evaluation and Research Methods*. 2d ed. Newbury Park, CA: Sage, 1990.

Sork, T. J., ed. *Mistakes Made and Lessons Learned: Overcoming Obstacles to Successful Program Planning*. New Directions for Adult and Continuing Education, no. 49. San Francisco: Jossey-Bass, 1991.

Steele, S. M. "The Evaluation of Adult and Continuing Education." In *Handbook of Adult and Continuing Education*, edited by S. B. Merriam and P. M. Cunningham, 260–72. San Francisco: Jossey-Bass, 1989.

Chapter VII

Professional Development in Continuing Education

Adult Educators:
Professionals with a Difference

As discussed in Chapter II, there is a long-standing debate within adult education over where the field is heading. In 1964, Webster Cotton noted that "perhaps the most pervasive criticism that can be made of adult educators is that we still do not know precisely *where* we are going, *why*, or *how best* to get there" (Cotton, quoted in Quigley, 1989, p. 1). Almost thirty years have passed but Cotton's remarks are still cogent. Adult educators remain divided over whether increasing professionalism will unify and strengthen the field, or whether it will further diminish its social reform tradition and isolate those working in the field who do not see themselves as adult educators.

Critics of professionalism argue convincingly that it emphasizes "schooling" over education and gives ascendency to technical skills. Others have argued that the traditional, authoritarian model of professionalism seems ill-suited to the participatory and democratic values that undergird adult education (Cervero, 1985).

This section is a "must read" if you don't really see what adult educators have in common with lawyers, dentists, physicians, engineers, architects, and others who are readily identified as professionals.

What I really like [about continuing education] is that it is fundamentally open-ended. The sky is the limit. As long as one can recover costs, one can do what one wants in a specific area. And I can't think of too many jobs that hold that out (Stacey).

"... It is not professionalization itself that threatens the field. Rather, it is a vision of professionalization that stresses such values as client dependence, professional authority, and rigidly defined criteria for the right to practice that has led many to be sceptical of adult education as a profession. It is my belief that professionalization is a desirable and even essential goal if adult and continuing education is to have a major impact on society in the coming century. In addition, I feel that it is crucial for us to create a professional vision that truly characterizes the strengths of our own field, rather than to follow blindly some existing model, such as that found in social work, law, or the health professions" (Brockett, 1991, p. 7).

Adult education is not what I do, it is what I am. . . . There is something special about what we are doing and I think we need to celebrate that. It is more than just what we do. For those of us who get enthused, it is part of who we are (Les).

In recent years, the focus of those who support professionalism has shifted from one of trying to see how adult education can adjust to the professional model to asking, "What kind of professional model will fit the needs of adult education?" Building on the work of Cervero and Schön (1987), Brockett (1991) suggests a model for professional practice that views practice as an art. "Professional artistry," to borrow Schön's term, describes the kinds of proficiencies that professionals require for competent practice in unique, uncertain, and contentious situations.[1] The essential elements of artistry are *technique* and *style.*

Technique includes the knowledge and skills that are required to successfully perform a task, such as planning a needs assessment or writing a brochure. These skills, which tend to be the focus of much training in adult education, are essential but they are not sufficient. Technical mastery, by itself, does not make one an adult educator.[2]

Style, according to Brockett, is the ingredient that turns the technician into the adult educator. Style is not easy to define or classify, but that is what distinguishes and elevates the work of the artist. It is style as much as technical skill that attracts us to Stevie Wonder or Toulouse-Lautrec. As Brockett describes it, "Style manifests itself in how one expresses oneself, which in turn is typically linked to such characteristics as personality, basic value system, and previous life experience" (1991, p. 9). Style can take many forms—compare Stevie Wonder to any number of other noteworthy musicians and composers—and though the merit of different styles is open to debate, there is no question that style goes beyond technical proficiency.

For the adult educator, style is founded on a personal philosophy of adult education, one that is informed by and, in turn, gives shape to practice. It is infused with both effective judgment (Cervero, 1989) and the craft knowledge (Kowalski, 1988) that comes with reflection on experience. It is characterized by dedication and commitment to the purposes of adult education. Style refers to the unique contribution that the adult educator

---

[1]   This would seem to offer an apt description of adult education given that every program opportunity and program setting has unique characteristics.

[2]   If you have read chapters II and III, you will recognize this refrain.

makes when all of these things are brought to bear in helping adults to learn within a specific context.

Professionalism, viewed in these terms, can accommodate education in many settings and for many purposes. It is not indispensably linked to formal training and credentials, it does not incorporate the implicit authoritarian relationships of the traditional model, and the concept of standards takes on a totally new meaning. Standards become defined by continuing educators in terms of the purposes of adult education and the settings and the context in which adult education occurs.

Professional Artistry: Technique and Style

The whole of this manual is devoted to drawing your attention to the areas of knowledge and the variety of skills that practitioners and theorists believe are required for effective adult education practice. Knox argued in 1979, and his views are supported by research with practitioners (Daniel and Rose, 1988; Rossman and Bunning, 1988), that adult educators need to be proficient or competent in three core areas.

1. The field of continuing education: This includes a knowledge of the agencies and organizations involved in adult education and, in particular, the organization that the adult educator works for (i.e., university continuing education and the specific university context); a knowledge of the historical and the global context; an understanding of the issues that affect the field; and an awareness of the resources that are available.

2. Adult development and learning: This includes knowledge about how adults learn (i.e., philosophies and theories); motivations for and barriers to learning and how learning relates to the life cycle; and facilitating learning.

3. Personal qualities and generic skills: These include all of the abilities and skills that enable adult educators to work effectively with others and that make their activities successful and innovative.

In addition, Knox looked at the roles and functions of adult educators and identified specific knowledge and skill components

The person that I feel is a good model for a continuing educator has a lot of energy and, coupled with that [she] demonstrates initiative and leadership, not in a formal leadership position, but [she] has some good ideas and [she] does something about them. [She] has the energy to do all of the things that need to be done and to cause things to happen. Not necessarily earth-shattering things but [she] will get an idea, initiate action, whatever that might be—call people together, meet, form the idea—and then sustain that effort. . . . [She] is really a good communicator, [she] has good contacts, and [she] seems to know what to do, when to do it, who to get on board, and how to work with the people that are necessary and critical in terms of making the program idea happen (Lee).

[He] is very knowledgeable about a content area and very confident about that . . . but [he] also has good process skills in going about the planning of something. [He] has very excellent recall for similar kinds of problems and issues that [he] has encountered, and [he] is able to draw from a lot of experience and a good deal of reading. [He] is able to bring those things to bear on a particular issue. I see it as a kind of research skill (Ronnie).

I really enjoy the creative side and working with other people to create things and figure out ways to do things (Francis).

The people that I know who are really good adult educators seem to thrive on change. They are creative, they are problem solvers, they don't like repetition, and they don't like routine. And the good thing about continuing education is that you can often avoid that (Les).

Communication within the unit is extremely important but it is easy to let that go. We are all frenetically going off in fifteen different directions. Yesterday and the day before, I couldn't keep up with myself, never mind communicate with anybody else, so it's very easy to assume that everyone knows what you're doing when, in fact, nobody does (Jan).

If I only had to develop programs in a narrow area, then things wouldn't be so complex as they are. But the programs that I develop cover everything from nursing to geology to a nondegree course on learning skills for new people coming in. I have to know a lot about a lot of things (Francis).

There is never a dull moment. There really isn't. It is extremely dynamic and almost frenetic sometimes. But even though I've told you that the phone calls and the demands on my time almost drive me crazy, that's also what makes it exciting for me. There is always something different going on (Chris).

for each. Program developers, for example, need to understand program development, the art and science of management, and the basics of consuming and producing research. Teachers of adults, on the other hand, need to have competence in the subject matter and in the teaching-learning process. There are other specific knowledge and skill requirements for counsellors and administrators.

The continuing educators who participated in the research for this manual agree with Knox. As a continuing educator, you require knowledge in all of the core and functional areas of practice. But the description of continuing education practice provided by continuing educators is much richer and more multifarious than anything described in the literature. While the latter focuses, understandably, on theory and how practice should unfold, continuing educators "tell it like it is," and in doing so, they emphasize the need for generic skills and abilities that barely get a passing nod in the textbooks.

In terms of the characteristics that they attribute to their work, continuing educators speak in one voice.

- Their work affords them considerable freedom and flexibility to pursue things that interest them and to set their own goals and directions. In this sense, continuing educators must be creative and entrepreneurial to make the most of the opportunities that are available to them.[3] If this characteristic has a downside, it is that some continuing educators find themselves relatively isolated from their colleagues and lacking the supports that they would like.

- Their work is extremely complex and the scope of their activities is often broad; much of what continuing educators need to know is contextually specific and must be learned on-the-job. Ironically, most of them learned by the seat of their pants, through trial and error, in CEUs that paid little or no attention to their orientation and subsequent development.

- The resources needed to do the job never seem adequate. Many continuing educators speak frankly and with evi-

---

[3]   Here entrepreneurial is used in the sense of being responsible for undertaking an enterprise. It is not tied to the notion of risk-taking for profit objectives.

dent frustration about the demands on their time, the lack of adequate administrative support, and the increasing pressure to make money.

In addition to the knowledge and skills related to continuing education practice and adult learning, continuing educators emphasize the following as crucial components of effective practice. Some of these have received attention in this manual, others have not, but they were raised often enough in the interviews to warrant their inclusion here.

- Time management skills: Time is short, the demands are heavy, and there is lots of detail. You have to develop strategies to organize your work and manage it effectively.

- Personal management skills: You will quickly discover that your job has no boundaries unless you impose them. Being committed to your work does not mean being swallowed up and consumed by it.

- Communication skills: As a continuing educator, you will spend considerable time talking to and working with people. You need effective presentation skills so that you can get your ideas across clearly and concisely; you need to feel comfortable speaking to all kinds of people and groups of all sizes; and you need good written skills. You will write proposals, needs-assessment and evaluation reports, letters and memos, and brochure copy. In all of your oral and written communication, you represent your university.

- Planning and processing skills: No one who reads this manual can miss the importance of planning and process to continuing education. Every aspect of program development involves planning and follow through, from the long-term, "big picture" look at where a program area is going to planning and follow through on an advisory committee meeting or a meeting with a faculty member.

- "People" or interpersonal skills: Communication skills are included here but so are the skills required to understand, empathize, and get along with others. The ability to be flexible and to compromise without losing sight of important goals or fundamental principles are key to

[Continuing education] is pretty challenging. It's open and it's flexible. Those are the things that I like. If you put in a lot of effort, you are going to get out a lot in return. . . . You can try just about anything as long as it is reasonable, as long as you can define it, and as long as it's within the broad parameters of where you work. It's very rare that you'll get bored. . . . You can really get yourself going and that is one of the disadvantages. You can get busy, busy, busy. You have to look at things and decide what is really important. Otherwise, you can get buried in some of this stuff (Gerry).

You can have several projects going at the same time and it's like you've got twenty things to do at once. But you still have to be able to concentrate on the big picture and make sure you get all the information and do everything for each project. And sometimes it seems like everything is pending—you are walking around with ten files and they are all pending and you can't get them off your desk. This one is waiting for something and this one is waiting for something. And it can be really difficult at times (Blair).

The Division is not a very cohesive unit and maybe that is true everywhere. There are so many activities and specialized program areas. So people work autonomously and, at times, it can be very difficult. Autonomy makes communication and a shared vision difficult (Jean).

143

It is important for people coming into this field to know that the demands on their time are going to be high. They are going to have to learn to prioritize and balance demands early. . . . One of the pieces of advice that I got from the personnel director was, the job is supposed to be done in this many hours per week and, yes, sometimes you have to do a few hours of overtime to get a project done—that's fine, that's expected. But if you can't do things in the expected length of time, given that you are giving it 110 percent of your time, there is too much work and somebody needs to be informed about this. . . . If you continue to do the work, people will look at that and say that the job is getting done and therefore it must be manageable. And you are tearing your hair out trying to meet deadlines and not asking for help. It's easier to do it yourself than to try and delegate because then you have to tell somebody how to do it. . . . But if you are going to give and give, you are going to burn out (Blair).

Sometimes one of our directors will say, "Gee, wouldn't it be great if all coordinators visited their classes at least once a year!" I have three hundred courses on the books. I work all day. I'm taking courses at night for my own edification—but now I'm supposed to work every night too? I'm not being critical but the demands can be pretty unrealistic (Andi).

establishing good interpersonal relationships.

- Learning skills: One of your greatest assets as a continuing educator will be your ability to reflect on and learn from your experiences in practice. Learning is vital to your development as an adult educator. If you are an inquisitive person who loves to learn (for any or all of the reasons Houle[4] identifies), continuing education is up to the challenge.

Avenues for Professional Development

The professional development of a continuing educator can occur in several ways. The typical routes involve:

1. academic study (certificate and degree programs)

2. in-service training and short courses

3. on-the-job training (including self-directed study).

Academic Study

Certificate and degree programs in adult education are offered by a number of Canadian universities.

A 1987 survey of Canadian educational institutions identified ten universities that offer graduate programs in adult education: the universities of Alberta, Calgary, Dalhousie, Guelph, New Brunswick, St. Francis Xavier, Saskatchewan, British Columbia, Montreal, and the Ontario Institute for Studies in Education (OISE). The last three institutions listed also offer doctoral programs in adult education (Wickett et al., 1987).

The results of the 1987 survey indicated that eight institutions offer certificate/diploma programs in adult education: the universities of Alberta, British Columbia, Calgary, Manitoba, Montreal, OISE, St. Francis Xavier, and Saskatchewan. Since 1987, a consortium of the universities of Alberta, Calgary, Manitoba, Saskatchewan, and Victoria has developed a Certificate in Adult and Continuing Education that is available through distance delivery.

A number of other institutions indicated that they offered

---

[4]   Chapter IV discusses motivations for participation in adult education.

degree credit courses in adult education that can be taken for credit toward general degrees in education.

In-service Training and Short Courses

In-service training refers to the short-term training that is done by the CEU, or by professional organizations like the Canadian Association for Continuing Education (CAUCE), which has a Professional Development Day as part of its annual general meeting and conference. There is no national data available on in-service training, but it seems safe to say, the opportunities available through this approach are limited.

Some institutions, such as the University of Alberta's Faculty of Extension, offer short-term continuing education programs to adult educators. These programs tend to focus very specifically on aspects of continuing education practice (for example, "How to Write Winning Proposals" or "Tips for Designing Effective Brochures").

Training that focuses on generic skills, like writing and presentation skills or time management, is the most readily available type of short-term training. Since this kind of training has wide appeal, it is generally available from a range of providers.

On-the-job Training and Self-directed Study

On-the-job training and self-directed study are the approaches used by most continuing educators, especially early in their careers, to develop their professional skills and competencies.

At the time that the interviews were conducted for this manual, none of the ten institutions represented had a formal orientation program or structured on-the-job training/mentoring/apprenticeship for new staff. As one Dean put it, orientation and training tend to be left in the hands of the supervisor with "hit and miss" results. From the comments of continuing educators who participated in this study, it appears to be mainly "miss." Most continuing educators describe their own learning as trial and error and flying by the seat of their pants. Without doubt, trial and error can result in significant learning experiences, but it can also be painful and frustrating for the continuing educator and others, including adult learners, who may be affected.

It is important to stress to a new [continuing educator] the benefits of goal setting and long-term planning because I think that it is very easy to get into a routine or to get so caught up in the day-to-day that we can't see beyond our noses (Morgan).

I'm not a perfectionist by any stretch of the imagination. I don't think I would survive if I was—which leads to another piece of advice. Recognize that there will be days when you'll feel that you are not accomplishing a darn thing. You're just doing all these bits and pieces of things.... Know that when you've had a day like this, very soon a day will follow when all kinds of things will fall together and the threads will get knotted and the bows will get tied and you'll be able to say, "My god, I got all this stuff tied up today!" (Les)

You have to be able to juggle all sorts of things at once. Somehow one's brain has to compartmentalize into, from very esoteric things—how to develop new things or solve difficult problems—to where are you going to set the coffee pot. Really, you have to do this balancing act (Jean).

There is simply never enough time to do all the things that have to be done. . . . So many of the activities that I should attend are in the evenings or at lunch hour, but I am only one body. And I am not prepared to give up every night and every noon hour in order to be working. So I try to find a balance (Jan).

An awful lot of the adult educators that I know . . . have dedicated their lives to the field. But a lot of them, and I was a perfect example of this, have no balance between work and home life. I had no family and there was nothing to keep me from becoming a workaholic. There was nothing to say that I had to go home and prepare a meal. So you end up working and all of a sudden it's 8:30 at night and you haven't had a decent meal in three days. . . . I am not married to the institution as I was before, but I really like my job and I am committed to doing the best job that I can (Blair).

[Continuing educators] need outstanding communication skills—verbal skills but also written skills. You have to be able to properly conceptualize and present your ideas. You can have good ideas, but if you can't articulate them, they sure won't make for good copy (Stacey).

Self-directed learning—I mean, it [has] become such a hackneyed cliche for us . . . but it is absolutely essential. I like to use as a metaphor for me that I am a roll with the sticky side out, and I am kind of indiscriminate in what I pick up. And that doesn't bother me because, invariably, I find that it comes in useful at some point in time. I find that no matter how I clutter myself up, at some point in time I am glad that I had that information to pull out (Jan).

To make your on-the-job experiences "pay off" as professional development, continuing educators offer the following advice.[5]

1. Find yourself a mentor or identify some role models within your CEU. These should be experienced people. Initiate discussion, ask for advice, get involved in a project they are working on, see if you can "tag along" to advisory committee meetings or other similar activities. Watch what they do, listen to what they say, and do not be afraid to ask them why.

2. Use your colleagues as resources. Ask questions and use others as sounding boards for your ideas.

3. Get involved in activities within your unit and within the university community. Volunteer—do not wait to be asked.

4. Spend time reflecting on your practice and on your beliefs and theories about adult education. Peters (1991, p. 91) offers a four-step approach to reflective practice (to which he applies the acronym DATA).

   Describe the problem, task, or incident that represents some critical aspect of practice needing examination and possible change.

   Analyze the nature of what is described, including the assumptions that support the actions taken to solve the problem, task, or incident.

   Theorize about alternative ways to approach the problem, task, or incident.

   Act on the basis of the theory.

Professional Reading

In addition to trying to make your work experiences meaningful professional development experiences, your growth as an adult educator requires that you become familiar with the general literature in adult education and in your area of special-

---

[5]   This advice should look familiar. Much of it has already been offered in earlier chapters.

ization (e.g., university continuing education and continuing professional education). Finding time to read is never easy, but it is necessary if you are to grow as an adult educator.

Each major section of each chapter within the manual contains a list of suggested readings. These readings were used to frame the discussion in the section and they will provide additional information on these topics. Most of these readings should be available in any university education library (and check the shelves of your CEU colleagues!). In addition, the citation for every source that is referred to in this manual is contained in the accompanying bibliography.

If you are looking for information on a specific topic, make use of the Educational Resources Information Centre (ERIC). ERIC is the major data base for adult education publications and is accessible by computer search through university education libraries. It contains references to North American publications and to a variety of international adult education publications.

The following list of selected periodicals will help you stay on top of the general field of adult education.

- *Adult Education Quarterly:* This is the major journal for the publication of research in adult education in North America. It is published by the American Association for Adult and Continuing Education (AAACE).

- *Adult Learning:* Also published by AAACE, this magazine is intended to provide useful information to practitioners. It comes out eight times per year.

- *The Canadian Journal for the Study of Adult Education:* This journal is published twice yearly by the Canadian Association for the Study of Adult Education (CASAE). It focuses on theory and research relevant to adult and continuing education. CASAE also publishes the proceedings of its annual research conference.

- *Canadian Journal of University Continuing Education:* Published twice yearly by the Canadian Association for University Continuing Education (CAUCE), this journal focuses on research and information that is useful to university continuing education practice.

- *Continuing Higher Education Review:* This journal of the

"Most observers of training in adult education would have to cite on-the-job experience as the major means through which practitioners become 'competent' or 'proficient.' As many have noted, most enter adult education through a 'back door' from some other field, role, or agency. Once in a continuing education or training position much needs to be learned quickly. Proficiency in the role thus develops through trial-and-error, through modelling another's behaviour, through consulting with colleagues and co-workers, and through self-directed study. Self-directed study is, of course, appropriate for those involved in a field that strives to assist adults in their own learning" (Merriam, 1988, p. 37).

We learn a lot of things fast and we practice them day in and day out, whether it is drafting a budget or designing a research instrument or doing a variety of things which require the acquisition of new skills. We have to learn how to learn and we have to know that part of our field quite well (Robin).

It seems so basic but it is definitely worth saying—when you come into this field, you have to take responsibility for your own learning. You have to find out what you need to know and how you can do things better. And I think that when you come into the field, you may not fully realize this (Andi).

I think that it is really important for people not to neglect their own growth as adult educators. I think . . . growth comes from reading, exposing oneself to different opportunities and conferences, and just generally through travel, through contacts with people, through networks . . . [through] getting plugged into what's happening world wide and having that network of people build up with whom one can communicate (Pat).

You know, as adult educators we know a lot about how people learn but we don't do any of that stuff. We know that it takes people a long time to understand even the basic components of their jobs and to feel comfortable with that. But we just put them in [their jobs] and they have to sink or swim. They are on their own, basically, which is unfortunate. . . . We haven't really thought about how complex this process is that we are engaged in (Gerry).

Because of my position, because of the things that I do, I've had very little time, although every year I say I'm going to do it, I have very little time to do background reading and research. And I feel very inadequate in very many ways. Maybe I sort of mask it when I deal with some of my colleagues, I don't know (Chris).

National University Continuing Education Association (NUCEA) is published three times per year. It is intended specifically for university continuing practitioners.

- *Convergence:* Published by the International Council for Adult Education (ICAE), this quarterly journal looks at developments in adult education around the world.

- *International Journal of Lifelong Education:* This quarterly journal provides an international forum for the discussion of theory and practice issues in lifelong education.

- *The Journal of Distance Education:* This journal is published twice yearly by the Canadian Association for Distance Education (CADE). It focuses on theory and practice in distance education.

- *Learning:* This is a publication of the Canadian Association for Adult Education (CAAE). Its focus is on adult education for citizenship and participation and it is intended for educators in all settings.

- *Proceedings of the Adult Education Research Conference (AERC):* These proceedings are published annually in conjunction with the Adult Education Research Conference.

- *New Directions for Adult and Continuing Education:* This is a quarterly series of source books that covers a broad range of adult education issues and settings. Each publication focuses on a specific theme which is explored from different perspectives that link theory and practice issues. (Formerly titled *New Directions for Continuing Education.*)

Include some adult education "classics" on your reading list. A few highly recommended classics are suggested below.[6]

- Brookfield, S. D. *Understanding and Facilitating Adult Learning.* San Francisco: Jossey-Bass, 1986. (A critical analysis of various topics related to the facilitation of adult learning.)

---

[6]   This list reflects the views of the author, and if anything can be said about it, it is that the list is incomplete. Ask your colleagues to provide other titles that they feel are a "must read." See also the list provided by Galbraith (1991, p. 203–7).

- Cross, K. P. *Adults as Learners*. San Francisco: Jossey-Bass, 1981. (An excellent review of adult-learning research prior to 1980.)

- Elias, J. L., and S. B. Merriam. *Philosophical Foundations of Adult Education*. Malabar, FL: Krieger, 1980. (An easy-to-read review of the major philosophical positions in adult education.)

- Jarvis, P. *Adult Learning in the Social Context*. London: Croom Helm, 1987. (A sociological look at adult learning.)

- Kidd, J. R. *How Adults Learn*. New York: Cambridge, 1973. (A classic written by one of Canada's best-known adult educators.)

- Knowles, M. S. *The Modern Practice of Adult Education: From Andragogy to Pedagogy*. New York: Cambridge, 1980. (A discussion of andragogy and its application to program development.)

- Lindeman, E. C. *The Meaning of Adult Education*. Norman, OK: Oklahoma Research Center for Continuing and Professional Education, 1989. (Originally published in 1926, this book emphasizes the importance of democratic values and the role of experience in adult education.)

- Tough, A. *The Adult's Learning Projects*. Toronto: Ontario Institute for Studies in Education, 1971. (Another Canadian publication that gained international recognition by focusing attention on the importance of self-directed learning in adulthood.)

Adult Education Associations

There are a number of professional associations and organizations for adult educators. Many of these publish journals and newsletters that are valuable resources for researchers and practitioners in the field (see the previous section in this chapter). In addition, these organizations sponsor conferences and other professional development activities that provide opportunities to meet adult educators with similar interests.

There are international, national, regional, and provincial

"A discipline for reading begins with the decision to read for professional development. Reading for professional development requires planning. Because too much literature is published each year for anyone to be able to keep up with it all, priorities have to be established. Prioritizing begins with identifying the kind of information that is needed. A time for reading professional literature has to be incorporated into the work schedule. For responsible professionals, reading is not a peripheral or optional activity" (Stubblefield, 1991, pp. 31–32).

"Reflective practice involves more than simply thinking about what one is doing and what one should do next. It involves identifying one's assumptions and feelings associated with practice, theorizing about how these assumptions and feelings are functionally or dysfunctionally associated with practice, and acting on the basis of the resulting theory of practice. In this sense, reflective practice involves critical thinking and learning, both of which are processes that can lead to significant self-development. . . . This means that the reflective practitioner is a student of his or her own actions and that the study of these actions is conducted in a systematic, analytical manner" (Peters, 1991, p. 89).

[The new continuing educator] should have a strong desire to learn new things, an openness to new approaches, and a willingness to experiment and take some risks with new approaches and new ways of doing things. I don't know if that is a skill, but it is an attitude that is essential in continuing education (Shawn).

When I think about [my new colleague], I think that there are lots of things that she could be doing to learn more about this place. She could be taking a couple of courses or getting involved in [the provincial adult education organization], finding out what the issues are. But I don't see her doing any of those things. I see her really running around like a chicken with its head cut off, trying to survive. So she still hasn't moved forward. . . . One of the reasons is that she isn't reading the stuff [i.e., the literature in adult education] and she isn't trying to get on top of the issues in the field (Gerry).

It is overly ambitious to expect all of us to develop [the skills] that we need in the first year or so. But [people need] a system for setting priorities to say which are the skills I should really focus on now, this year, and next year. Again, planning our own progress in developing these skills might be a good tool (Robin).

associations for adult educators. Some of these have broad membership appeal, such as the Canadian Association for Adult Education (CAAE) and the Canadian Association for Studies in Adult Education (CASAE). Others, such as the Canadian Association for University Continuing Education (CAUCE), are specifically intended for those of us working in university continuing education.[7] There are also special interest groups such as the Canadian Association for Distance Education (CADE) and others that are specific to areas of practice (Teaching English as a Second Language, TESL), as well as regional and provincial adult education associations.

Ask your colleagues about the provincial, regional, and special interest associations that are relevant to your situation. If there are opportunities for membership and/or participation, take advantage of these.

Developing a Professional Development Plan

Given the emphasis that is placed on planning and managing in this manual, the suggestion that you should develop a personal plan for professional development will come as no surprise. In fact, planning and managing your own professional development program may be one of the first adult education programs over which you assume responsibility. Chapters V and VI discuss program development in detail and many of these principles apply to planning for professional development.

In developing a professional development plan, Brockett (1991) emphasizes four themes that are central to professional development. These same themes provided much of the framework for the development of this manual.

1. The importance of self-awareness: Understanding our own value systems, our strengths and weaknesses, and the assumptions on which we base our behaviour is critical to our development as adult educators. Critical reflection allows us to transform both our theory and our practice and to develop our professional style.

---

[7] Your CEU probably holds an institutional membership in CAUCE and receives copies of its publications and notification of its annual conference. The conference provides an excellent networking opportunity for university practitioners.

2. The value of professional literature: Our theory and practice are informed and enriched by contemporary and historical writings in the field as well as by the theory and practice of adult educators around the globe.

3. The link between professional development and making a contribution to professional practice: Professional development involves an exchange among professionals. Involvement in professional associations is an important way to develop networks and to share ideas and insights that will benefit others working in the field.

4. The importance of taking a proactive approach to professional development: Since much of what we need to know we learn once we are on-the-job, a proactive approach to self-development (i.e., one that accepts that the responsibility for learning rests with each of us) is a powerful, and perhaps essential, tool for our development as continuing educators.

I found myself reinventing "Time Text" [a time-management calendar], only I'm sure they would never approve of the categories I'm using. I got myself a three-ring binder and some subject dividers and I use it for planning and keeping track of what I have to do today and next week. So I have two categories for my planning. . . . Then I divided the rest of the binder into sections that refer to programs. There is one for notes about the [name of] program. These are not things that I am going to do tomorrow or next week but things that I will do for the next session (Les).

Questions to Ask

1. What opportunities and/or supports are available from your university for part-time academic study in adult education? For in-service and short-term training?

2. In which professional associations (national, regional, provincial) does it seem important for you to become involved?

3. How will you go about assessing and prioritizing your own needs for professional development?

   A suggestion for doing this assessment follows (adapted from Lund and McGechaen, 1981, p. 128–29):

   - Use this manual as a guide for identifying knowledge and skill requirements for practice. You should also discuss knowledge and skill requirements with your supervisor and other colleagues in your CEU.

   - Determine how important each skill or knowledge component is to your performance as a continuing educator (use a ranking system of 0–3, where 0 = not important, and 3 = very important).

Sometimes [the director] will ask us to review a program proposal or an evaluation proposal and I'll look at it and it looks fine to me. Then someone else in the room will start to pick out all of these things and ask questions and I think, "Oh gee, that's right," but I never would have thought about those things (Rene).

Note: This quote is from someone who is new to continuing education.

You definitely have to have good interpersonal skills. You have to deal with so many types of people—students, instructors, staff, the general public. Each person has to feel like their problems or concerns are important to you and that you are interested—even if they are the tenth person to phone that morning and they are complaining about something that you think is pretty insignificant (Sandy).

I equate what I have learned this year to when you finally get your driver's licence. You know all the stuff about driving a car but you really don't learn to drive until that first day when you get in the car by yourself and you go to switch lanes but you forget to look and you almost get side-swiped. That is when you learn to drive. I mean that's what has happened to me here . . . . A lot of it is just going out there and forgetting to shoulder check and almost getting side swiped. And don't let that opportunity pass you by to sit back and say what does this mean? What can I do next time? I've been making mental notes all year and writing them down in one section [of a file] called "ideas" and some of those things are reflected in this year's program (Les).

Note: This quote is from someone who earned an M.Ed. in adult education before entering continuing education.

- Assess your own skill/knowledge level for each item you have identified (use a ranking system of 0–3, where 0 = no improvement needed or not applicable, and 3 = much improvement required).

- When you have ranked all the items, enter them into a chart like the one that follows and total your scores (for each item, add the two rankings together).

- Items that total 6 or 5 are high-priority items for professional development. These are the skills/knowledge that you need to develop in the short term. Those items that are ranked 4 or 3 should be scheduled into your longer-term planning for professional development.

- Plan how you intend to increase your proficiency in the skill/knowledge areas that you have identified and get going!

- Review your self-assessment and adjust your development plan on a regular basis.

Skill/Knowledge Self-Assessment

Skills/Knowledge Component	Importance				Improvement				Total
	0= Not Important	1 = Somewhat important	2 = Important	3 = Very Important	0 = No improvement needed	1 = A little improvement needed	2 = Improvement needed	3 = Much imrovement needed	
1. Meeting skills				3		1			4
2. Have a personal philosophy of adult ed.				3				3	6
3.									

152

Suggested Readings

Brockett, R. G., ed. *Professional Development for Educators of Adults*. New Directions For Adult and Continuing Education, no. 51. San Francisco: Jossey-Bass, 1991.

Cervero, R. M. "Becoming More Effective in Everyday Practice." In *Fulfilling the Promise of Adult and Continuing Education*, edited by B. A. Quigley, 107–14. New Directions for Continuing Education, no. 44, San Francisco: Jossey-Bass, 1989.

Appendix

Summary of Philosophies

(Hiemstra, 1988, p. 183–84)

Idealism

Meaning: The overall meaning of life is in life itself

What is Reality: Divine or absolute truths

Nature of Humanness: Each of us is a part of the meaning

Educational Aims: Tell others the truths

Educational Method: Inductive reasoning; authority lecturing

Educational Content: Life's events; the world of our own mind

Main Criticism: "Truths" may be only in beholder's eyes

Key Proponents: Plato (Cushman, 1958; Taylor, 1926)

Programs/Practices: Some religious education programs

Realism

Meaning: Empirically proven facts; reality

What is Reality: Natural Laws and facts

Nature of Humanness: Awareness is perceiving
Educational Aims: Develop intellectual abilities
Educational Method: Inductive and Scientific reasoning
Educational Content: Life's laws and principles
Main Criticism: Empirical facts always subject to change
Key Proponents: Chisholm (1961); Whitehead (1933)
Programs/Practices: Phenomenology; science education

Progressivism

Meaning: Concrete facts and interrelationships
What is Reality: Theory is based on truth
Nature of Humanness: Humans are part of the environment
Educational Aims: Development through experiencing
Educational Method: Problem solving; experiential method
Educational Content: Building on people's experiences and needs
Main Criticism: Diminishes traditional role of teacher
Key Proponents: Bergevin (1967); Dewey (1938); Lindeman (1926)
Programs/Practices: Adult Basic Education; community education; Cooperative Extension

Liberalism

Meaning: Freedom comes through a liberated mind
What is Reality: Humans endowed with ability to reason
Nature of Humanness: Improvement through intellect and wisdom
Educational Aims: Development of the mind
Educational Method: Critical reading; teacher as expert
Educational Content: History; humanities; the classics
Main Criticism: Past may not relate to modern problems
Key Proponents: Aristotle (Bambrough, 1963); Hutchins (1968)
Programs/Practices: Chautauqua; Elderhostel; Great Books; Lyceum; Center for the Study of Liberal Education for Adults

Behavioralism

Meaning: Human behavior tied to prior conditioning

What is Reality: External forces control human behavior

Nature of Humanness: Stimulus creates response

Educational Aims: Behavioral change; develop behavioral skills

Educational Method: Conditioning; feedback; practice

Educational Content: Life skills; basic skills

Main Criticism: Learning too complex for behavioral control

Key Proponents: Skinner (1971); Tyler (1949)

Programs/Practices: Adult Performance Level; behavior modification; behavioral objectives

Humanism

Meaning: Intellect distinguishes humans and animals

What is Reality: Humans have potential and innate goodness

Nature of Humanness: Dignity, freedom, and autonomy are sacred

Educational Aims: Individual potentiality; self-actualization

Educational Method: Self-direction; teamwork; facilitation

Educational Content: Any curriculum a vehicle for meeting needs

Main Criticism: Important societal goals can be missed

Key Proponents: Knowles (1980); Maslow (1976); Rogers (1969); Tough (1979)

Programs/Practices: Individualized learning efforts; learning projects; sensitivity training

Radicalism

Meaning: People create meaning, history, and culture

What is Reality: Knowledge leads to understanding of reality

Nature of Humanness: Humans can change their environment

Educational Aims: Create change through education/knowledge

Educational Method: Dialogue and Problem Solving

Educational Content: Begin with cultural situations of learners

APPENDIX

Main Criticism: Tends to be idealistic in nature
Key Proponents: Adams (1975); Freire (1970); Illich (1970)
Programs/Practices: Community-based literacy; Freire's literacy
    training; Highlander Centre

Unlike traditional philosophies, which make normative statements about what should be, *analytic philosophy* is concerned with the clarification of ideas, arguments, and statements of policy (Elias and Merriam, 1980). For example, analytic philosophers have analyzed such troublesome concepts as adult (Paterson, 1979), adult education and the education of adults (Lawson,1975), and needs (Monette, 1979). Through an analysis of how terms are used, analytic philosophers attempt to arrive at philosophically sound concepts.

Personal Philosophy Worksheet

(Hiemstra, 1988, p. 187)

Philosophical Beliefs

Philosophical System:

Meaning:

What is Reality?:

Nature of Being Human:

Professional Practice

Educational Aim:

Educational Method:

Educational Content:

Four Orientations to Learning

Aspect	Behaviourist	Cognitivist	Humanist	Social Learning
Learning theorists	Thorndike, Pavlov, Watson, Guthrie, Hull, Tolman, Skinner	Koffka, Kohler, Lewin, Piaget, Ausubel, Bruner, Gagne	Maslow, Rogers	Bandura, Rotter
View of the learning process	Change in behavior	Internal mental process (including insight, information processing, memory, perception)	A personal act to fulfill potential	Interaction with and observation of others in a social context
Focus of learning environment	Stimuli in external structuring	Internal cognitive needs	Affective and cognitive	Interaction of person, behavior, and environment
Purpose of education	Produce behavioral change in desired direction	Develop capacity and skills to learn better	Become self-actualized, autonomous	Model new roles and behavior
Teacher's role	Arranges environment to elicit desired response	Structures content of learning activity	Facilitates development of whole person	Models and guides new roles and behavior
Manifestation in adult learning	• Behavioral objectives • Competency-based education • Skill development and training	• Cognitive development • Intelligence, learning, and memory as function of age • Learning how to learn	• Andragogy • Self-directed learning	• Socialization • Social roles • Mentoring • Locus of control

(Merriam and Caffarella, 1991, p. 138)

Mid-Course Evaluation*

Questions 1 to 7 will require you to circle the appropriate response. (Note: "1" always means "not at all" while "5" always means "completely.") Questions 8 and 9 ask for your written comments.

1. Are the learning objectives clearly stated for the course?

1	2	3	4	5
Not at all				Completely

2. Do you think that the course will contribute to the overall knowledge and skills you hoped the program would provide?

1	2	3	4	5

3. Does the course have relevance to your work (your job)?

1	2	3	4	5

4. Is your instructor well organized?

1	2	3	4	5

5. Does your instructor draw on the work and life experiences of students to enrich learning in the course?

1	2	3	4	5

6. Is your instructor able to illustrate practical applications of the course material?

1	2	3	4	5

7. Has your instructor planned a challenging but not burdensome workload?

1	2	3	4	5

8. Comments concerning the course.

9. Comments concerning the instructor.

---

* This evaluation form, used by the Management Studies section of The University of Manitoba's Continuing Education Division, is intended to provide students with an opportunity to give feedback to the instructor while the course is in progress. Used with permission of the Continuing Education Division, The University of Manitoba.

Course Evaluation Questionnaire*

Introduction

We sincerely hope you have found this course to be of value and a benefit to you. We would like your assistance in completing this evaluation so that we can continue to improve our programs. Your comments and suggestions will be appreciated, and your reply is confidential. It is not necessary to sign your name.

Instructions

Please use a soft-lead pencil to answer the first seventeen questions, using the computer-coded answer sheet provided. **Be sure to put the course name/number and the instructor's name on the IBM answer sheet.** Each question asks you to reply, based on a scale ranging from 1 to 5. For example:

7.   This instructor was well organized.
        1   2   3   4   5
        ] [   ] [   ] [   ] [   ] [
    Not at all   Completely

Fill in the small numbered column which most accurately reflects your opinion, checking that the number of the question/statement on the questionnaire corresponds with the item/line number on the answer sheet. This completed form is machine-read, so please be careful in making any erasures in order to avoid confusing the computer!

    Remember, the reply "1" always means "**not at all,**" while "5" always means "**completely.**"

Questions 18 to 22 require a written response. Please consider carefully your experience in this course in responding to these questions.

    Please return the questionnaire with the computer-coded sheet to the person administering the evaluation or mail to the Continuing Education Office:

Management Studies Section
Continuing Education Division
University of Manitoba
188 Continuing Education Complex
Winnipeg, Manitoba
R3T 2N2

---

*   Used with permission of the Continuing Education Division, The University of Manitoba.

APPENDIX

Course Content

The following questions relate to the subject matter of the course you have just completed. When answering these questions, you should make every effort to separate the content of the course from the instruction (or teaching) you received. Content refers to the relevance, comprehensiveness, and usefulness of the course material.

1. Were learning objectives clearly stated for the course?

2. Did the course meet your personal learning objectives (expectations)?

3. Did this course contribute to the overall knowledge and skills you hoped the program would provide?

4. Did the course have relevance to your work (your job)?

5. Did you find the textbook/handouts useful as a learning resource?

Instruction

Instructors may vary in style and in the learning techniques each employs. As much as possible, try not to compare this instructor with others but assess how effectively he or she was in helping you master the course content.

Name of Instructor:

6. Was effective in creating a stimulating learning experience?

7. Drew on the work and life experiences of students to enrich learning in the course?

8. Was able to illustrate practical applications of the course material?

9. Integrated textbook/handout materials in classroom presentations?

10. Was able to refer individual students to additional study aids or job-related resources?

11. Planned a challenging but not burdensome workload?

12. Provided clear, helpful feedback on in-class exercises, assignments, and tests?

13. Provided prompt feedback on assignments and tests?

14. Was well organized?

15. Communicated clear marking criteria/procedures?

16. Informed students promptly of important deadlines and changes in the schedule?

Administration

Administration refers to the co-ordination of the course/program by the Continuing Education Division.

17. Were Continuing Education Staff friendly and informative when responding to course or administrative inquiries? If you had no contact with Continuing Education Staff please check here

Additional Comments

Questions 18 to 22 provide you with an opportunity to reflect on the course and comment on your learning, the course content, instruction, and administration.

18. Please describe a significant learning experience for you in the course.

19. Comments concerning the course content.

20. Comments concerning the instructor.

21. Comments concerning the administration of the course.

22. Would you recommend this course to others? Please explain.

CONTINUING EDUCATION BUDGET/COURSE PROPOSAL

PLEASE PRESS FIRMLY - YOU ARE MAKING THREE COPIES

COURSE # _____ TITLE _____ DEPT. # _____

TYPE _____ TECHNIQUE _____ LENGTH (Hrs) _____ TERM: R F W I S. 19 _____

FROM ____ / ____ / ____ TO ____ / ____ / ____ CANCELLATION DATE ____ / ____ / ____
　　　yy　　mm　　dd　　　　yy　　mm　　dd　　　　　　　　　　　　　yy　　mm　　dd

ENROL: MAX _____ MIN _____ START TIME: _____ END TIME _____
　　　　　　　　　　　　　　　　　　　　　　　24 hour clock　　　　　　24 hour clock

LOCATION: ROOM _____ BUILDING _____ PARKING LOT _____

TEXT _____

INSTRUCTOR NAME: 1/ _____ 2/ _____ 3/ _____
　　　　　　　　　　　(ATTACH PAYROLL INFORMATION FORM)

FEES: EARLY _____ REG _____ LATE _____ GRP _____ STU/SR _____ NON/TUITION _____

CERTIFICATE COURSE Y/N ☐ (IF NO ATTACH GST FORM)　　GST APPLICABLE Y/N ☐

PROPOSED BY: _____ APPROVED BY: _____ DATE: _____

NOTES	EXPENSES	
EARLY REG DATE: ____ / ____ / ____	150	ACADEMIC SALARIES	_____

NOTES

EARLY REG DATE: ____ / ____ / ____
　　　　　　　　yy　　mm　　dd

SALARY:

____ X ____ = ____ X $ ____ = $ ____
mtgs.　duration　hrs.　　rate　　total

HTR $ _____

INCOME

REGS _____ X FEE $ _____ = $ _____

REGS _____ X FEE $ _____ = $ _____

REGS _____ X FEE $ _____ = $ _____

OTHER INCOME / GRANTS　　　　$ _____

　　　　TOTAL INCOME:　　　$ _____

　　　　NET INCOME:　　　　$ _____

　　　INCOME / EXPENSE RATIO:　% _____

White - Department
Yellow - Finance
Green - Program Area

EXPENSES

150	ACADEMIC SALARIES	_____
670	GUEST LECTURERS	_____
190	SPECIAL ACADEMIC SALARIES	_____
225	SUPPORT STAFF	_____
400 / 405	TRAVEL ACADEMIC/DUTY TRAVEL	_____
475	MEMBERSHIPS	_____
477	RECEPTIONS	_____
480	TEACHING MATERIALS	_____
565	BOOKS & SUBSCRIPTIONS	_____
572	RENTALS	_____
600	GENERAL SUPPLIES/EXPENSES	_____
636	ENTERTAINMENT	_____
651	TELEPHONE - LONG DISTANCE	_____
654	PRINTING SERVICES - BROCHURES	_____
655 / 656	PRINTING SERVICES - DUPLICATING	_____
657	DEPARTMENT PHOTOCOPYING	_____
658	POSTAGE	_____
665	ADVERTISING	_____
667	REGISTRATION COSTS	_____
	TOTAL EXPENSE:	$ _____

April '92

This form is used by the Continuing Education Division at The University of Manitoba. Only the direct costs associated with delivering an educational event are captured on this form. Revenue forecasts are also entered here. The net income figure and the income/expense ratio help to identify the contribution that the event will make to indirect costs. The Continuing Education Division expects its nondegree programs (overall, not individually) to recover all direct costs as well as the indirect costs borne by the Division. The Division is not responsible for such things as rent on campus facilities, heating and lighting, or building maintenance and repairs. Used with permission of the Continuing Education Division, The University of Manitoba.

Brochure Preparation Checklist[1]

(adapted from Leffel, 1983)

Before You Start

1. Who is your intended audience? What are their major desires and needs?
2. What are the benefits of attendance?
3. What types of information will all members of the audience need to make an enrollment decision?
4. What special features, if any, does the program have?
5. Would testimonials be helpful? Are they available?
6. Will photographs be used to demonstrate a program feature? Are the photos available or have arrangements been made to have them taken?
7. What is your timetable for writing and printing the brochure? How far in advance of the event will potential participants receive the brochure (minimum 6 weeks)? What is the printer's estimate of delivery after receiving the copy?
8. Would it be helpful to involve a designer early in the preparation of your brochure?

Writing Copy

1. Does the title communicate the intent and benefit of the course?
2. Should the intended audience be stated as part of the title?
3. What is the date of the program? Is the length or format a special feature?
4. Who is the sponsoring agency(s)?
5. Are there members of an advisory committee who should be listed?
6. Who should attend the program?

---

[1] Brochure Preparation Checklist from "Designing Brochures for Results," by L. G. Leffel, 1983, pp. 35–37. Permission granted to excerpt by the Learning Resources Network, 1550 Haynes Drive, Manhattan, KS 66502 © LERN.

7. Should attendees have any prior knowledge or skills?

8. Is the program a follow-up to a previous program?

9. What are the programs benefits? Are they stated in short, concise statements?

10. What is the sponsoring agency's capability?

11. What will be taught? Will the description provide the detail required? Will it encourage reader involvement?

12. What is the time schedule?

13. What are the instructors' or speakers' qualifications to teach this specific program?

14. What instructional strategies will be used—are these a special feature?

15. What instructional materials will be used—are these a special feature?

16. What do past participants say about this program if it has been offered previously?

17. What companies or agencies have previously participated?

18. How is the location attractive to the audience? What are the parking/travel directions?

19. What is the fee and what does it include? Can the fee be a special feature? How about any restrictions that may apply to a refund? Are there late penalties or early registration discounts? What about GST?

20. How do participants pay—by cheque, credit card? In full, by installment? Can they be invoiced?

21. How do participants register—by mail, phone, FAX, in person? Is there a registration deadline?

22. How do they make lodging reservations, if required?

23. What forms should be provided? How can they be made easy to complete? Should any other information be collected?

24. Who should be contacted for additional information?

25. What types of credit may be earned? Will a certificate be provided? Is this a special feature?

26. Is it appropriate to try to sell the program on an in-house basis?

27. Should future programs of interest be listed?

28. Would a note about tax deduction for educational expenses be helpful?

29. Would a note to route the brochure be helpful? Should the route request include a statement that several mailing lists were used and duplicates may be received?

30. Is "you" and "your" used to encourage reader involvement?

31. Are active verbs and phrases used?

32. Have captions been written for photos?

33. Will a mailing panel be needed?

Preparing the Copy

1. What is the best format to use with your information?

2. How should the information be placed to lead the reader?

3. What information should be highlighted? Have notes been made in the margins of the typed copy noting suggestions for highlighting?

4. Has a major benefit been identified for the cover and mail panel? Does the cover include all the necessary information? Does it identify the sponsoring agency?

5. Will the information fit in the dummy layout? Should any alterations in format or information be made? Has provision been made for "white" space? Are you sure the information will not have a crowded appearance? Will your typeface point size be readable?

6. Will the brochure fit standardized envelopes? Is the size economical for mailing?

7. Will the mail panel be returned with the registration form? (This is useful for tracking different mailing lists.)

8. What paper and ink colours should be used to create the desired effect?

9. How will design and artwork be used to complement the copy? If an illustration will be used, does it depict a benefit? Do you need professional assistance?

10. Have you involved a disinterested party to review your ideas?

11. How many copies will you need?

12. What is the estimated cost of the brochure? Of mailings?

13. Who will be responsible for final sign off?
14. Has provision been made for labels, envelopes, scheduling, etc., to insure that the brochure will be mailed on time?

Reviewing the Final Brochure

1. Does the overall appearance of the brochure create the pleasing effect you anticipated?
2. Does the appearance create the impression of quality you anticipated?
3. Does the information quickly involve and lead the reader?
4. What suggestions would you make for improvements next time? Who should be involved in reviewing the final product—colleague? participant?
5. Did calls for information from potential participants reflect any weaknesses in the information provided? (Make sure you check this with the staff who handle most of the calls.)
6. Did you achieve your enrolment projects?

Bibliography

Apps, J. W. 1985. *Improving practice in continuing education*. San Francisco: Jossey-Bass.

Bains, G. 1985. A profile of adult educators in Canadian universities. *Canadian Journal of University Continuing Education,* 11(2): 12–26.

Barer-Stein, T., and Draper, J. A., eds. 1988. *The craft of teaching adults*. Toronto: OISE Press.

Beatty, P. T.; Benefield, L. L.; and Linhart, L. S. 1991. Evaluating the teaching and learning process. In *Facilitating adult learning: A transactional process,* ed. M. W. Galbraith, 163–92. Malabar, FL: Robert E. Krieger.

Beder, H. 1986. *Marketing continuing education*. New Directions for Continuing Education, no. 31. San Francisco: Jossey-Bass.

———. 1989. Purposes and philosophies of adult education. In *Handbook of adult and continuing education,* ed. S. B. Merriam and P. M. Cunningham, 37–50. San Francisco: Jossey-Bass.

Bee, H. L. 1987. *The journey of adulthood*. New York: Macmillan.

Bhola, H. 1989. *World trends and issues in adult education*. London: Jessica Kingsley.

BIBLIOGRAPHY

Blackwood, C. C., and White, B. A. 1991. Technology for teaching and learning improvement. In *Facilitating adult learning: A transactional process,* ed. M. W. Galbraith, 135–62. Malabar, FL: Robert E. Krieger.

Blakely, R. 1957. The path and the goal. *Adult Education,* 7(2): 93–98.

Blaney, J. P. 1986. Cultural conflict and leadership in extension. *Canadian Journal of University Continuing Education,* 12(1): 70–78.

Boone, E. J. 1985. *Developing programs in adult education.* Englewood Cliffs, NJ: Prentice-Hall.

Boshier, R. 1971. Motivational orientations of adult education participants: A factor analytic exploration of Houle's typology. *Adult Education,* 21: 3–26.

Boshier, R., and Collins, J. 1985. The Houle typology after twenty-two years: A large scale empirical test. *Adult Education Quarterly,* 35(3): 113–30.

Boyle, P. G. 1981. *Planning better programs.* New York: McGraw-Hill.

Brackhaus, B. 1984. Needs assessment in adult education: Its problems and prospects. *Adult Education Quarterly,* 34(4): 223–39.

Brim, O. G., and Ryff, C. D. 1980. On the properties of life events. In *Life-span development and behavior: Vol. 3.,* ed. R. Baltes and O. G. Brim. New York: Academic Press.

Brockett, R. G., ed. 1988. *Ethical issues in adult education.* New York: Teachers College Press.

————. 1991. *Professional development for educators of adults.* New Directions for Adult and Continuing Education, no. 51. San Francisco: Jossey-Bass.

Brooke, W. M., and Morris, J. F. 1987. *Continuing education in Canadian universities: A summary report of policies and practices - 1985.* Ottawa: Canadian Association for University Continuing Education.

Brookfield, S. D. 1986. *Understanding and facilitating adult learning.* San Francisco: Jossey-Bass.

———. 1987. *Developing critical thinkers: Challenging adults to explore alternative ways of thinking and acting.* San Francisco: Jossey-Bass.

———. 1990. *The skillful teacher.* San Francisco: Jossey-Bass.

Brumfield, L. L., and Nesbit, D. P. 1979. Supervision and monitoring. In *Attracting able instructors of adults,* ed. M. A. Brown and H. G. Copeland, 39–50. New Directions for Continuing Education, no. 4. San Francisco: Jossey-Bass.

Brundage, D. H., and MacKeracher, D. 1980. *Adult learning principles and their application to program planning.* Toronto: Ontario Ministry of Education.

Burnham, B. R. 1988. Program planning as technology in three adult education organizations. *Adult Education Quarterly,* 38(4): 211–23.

Burns, J. H., and Roche, G. A. 1988. Marketing for adult educators: Some ethical questions. In *Ethical issues in adult education,* ed. R. G. Brockett, 51–63. New York: Teachers College Press.

Calvert, J. C. 1989. Instructional design for distance learning. In *Instructional design: New alternatives for effective education and training,* ed. K. A. Johnson and L. J. Foa, 92–105. New York: Macmillan.

Cameron, C. R. 1981. Certification should be established. In *Examining controversies in adult education,* ed. B. W. Kreitlow and Associates, 72–83. San Francisco: Jossey-Bass.

Campbell, D. 1984. *The new majority: Adult learners in the university.* Edmonton: The University of Alberta Press.

Canadian Association for Adult Education. 1982. *From the adult's point of view.* Toronto: Canadian Association for Adult Education.

Canadian Association for University Continuing Education. 1992. *Handbook 1992.* Toronto: Ryerson Polytechnical Institute.

Canadian Chamber of Commerce, Focus 2000. 1990. *Business-education partnerships: Your planning process guide.* Ottawa: Canadian Chamber of Commerce.

Cassara, B. B., ed. 1990. *Adult education in a multicultural society.* London: Routledge.

Cassidy, F., and Faris, R., eds. 1987. *Choosing our future: Adult education and public policy in Canada.* Toronto: OISE Press.

Cauthers, J. 1991. Continuing education in the learning society: An interview with Dr. Jerold Apps. *Canadian Journal of University Continuing Education*, 17(2): 55–68.

Cervero, R. M. 1985. The predicament of professionalism for adult education. *Adult Literacy and Basic Education*, 9(1): 11–17.

————. 1988. *Effective continuing education for professionals.* San Francisco: Jossey-Bass.

————. 1989. Becoming more effective in everyday practice. In *Fulfilling the promise of adult and continuing education*, ed. B. A. Quigley, 107–14. New Directions for Continuing Education, no. 44. San Francisco: Jossey-Bass.

Clark, B. R. 1983. *The higher education system.* Berkeley: University of California Press.

Coady, M. M. 1939. *Masters of their own destiny.* New York: Harper & Row.

Cohen, M. D., and March, J. G. 1974. *Leadership and ambiguity: The American college president.* New York: McGraw-Hill.

Conti, G. J. 1985. The relationship between teaching style and adult student learning. *Adult Education Quarterly*, 35(4): 220–28.

————. 1990. Identifying your teaching style. In *Adult learning methods: A guide for effective instruction,* ed. M. W. Galbraith, 79–96. Malabar, FL: Robert E. Krieger.

Cookson, P. S. 1989. International and comparative adult education. In *Handbook of adult and continuing education*, ed. S. B. Merriam and P. M. Cunningham, 70–83. San Francisco: Jossey-Bass.

Coombs, P. 1985. *The world crisis in education: The view from the eighties.* New York: Oxford Press.

Courtney, S. 1989. Defining adult and continuing education. In *Handbook of adult and continuing education,* ed. S. B. Merriam and P. M. Cunningham, 15–25. San Francisco: Jossey-Bass.

Cranton, P. 1989. *Planning instruction for adult learners.* Toronto: Wall and Thompson.

Cross, K. P. 1979. Adult learners: Characteristics, needs, and interests. In *Lifelong learning in America: An overview of current practices, available resources, and future prospects,* ed. R. E. Peterson & Associates. San Francisco: Jossey-Bass.

————. 1981. *Adults as learners: Increasing participation and facilitating learning.* San Francisco: Jossey-Bass.

Cruikshank, J. 1991. University extension: How can we recapture the vision. *Canadian Journal of University Continuing Education,* 17(1): 21–37.

Culleton, B. 1983. *In search of April Raintree.* Winnipeg, MB: Pemmican.

Cunningham, P. M. 1988. The adult educator and social responsibility. In *Ethical issues in adult education,* ed. G. Brockett, 133–45. New York: Teachers College Press.

————. 1989. Making a more signficant impact on society. In *Fulfilling the promise of adult and continuing education,* ed. B. A. Quigley, 33–46. New Directions for Continuing Education, no. 44. San Francisco: Jossey-Bass.

Cyert, R. M. 1985. Academic leadership. *Continuum,* 49(2): 123–28.

Daniel, R., and Rose, H. 1988. Comparative study of adult education practitioners and professors on future knowledge and skills needed by adult educators (1982). In *Training educators of adults: The theory and practice of graduate adult education,* ed. S. D. Brookfield, 168–81. New York: Routledge.

Darkenwald, G. G., and Merriam, S. B. 1982. *Adult education: Foundations of practice.* New York: Harper & Row.

Darkenwald, G. G., and Valentine, T. 1985. Factor structure of deterrents to public participation in adult education. *Adult Education Quarterly,* 35(4): 177–93.

Deshler, D., ed. 1984. *Evaluation for program improvement.* New Directions for Continuing Education, no. 24. San Francisco: Jossey-Bass.

BIBLIOGRAPHY

Devereaux, M. S. 1984. *One in every five: A survey of adult education in Canada*. Ottawa: Statistics Canada and Department of the Secretary of State.

Dewey, J. 1938. *Experience and education*. New York: Macmillan.

DiDilvestro, F. R., ed. 1981. *Advising and counselling adult learners*. New Directions for Continuing Education, no. 10. San Francisco: Jossey-Bass.

Dominick, J. E. 1990. How program developers make decisions in practice. *Proceedings of the 31st Annual Adult Education Research Conference*, 31 (May): 71–76.

Elias, J. L., and Merriam, S. B. 1980. *Philosophical foundations of adult education*. Malabar, FL: Robert E. Krieger.

Erikson, E. H. 1982. *The lifecycle completed: A review*. New York: Norton.

Ewert, D. M. 1989. Adult education and international development. In *Handbook of adult and continuing education*, ed. S. B. Merriam and P. M. Cunningham, 84–98. San Francisco: Jossey-Bass.

Faris, R. 1975. *The passionate educators*. Toronto: Peter Martin.

Freedman, L. 1987. *Quality in continuing education*. San Francisco: Jossey-Bass.

Freire, P. 1970. *Pedagogy of the oppressed*. New York: Herder & Herder.

Gagne, R. M.; Briggs, L. J.; and Wager, W. W. 1992. *Principles of instructional design*. 4th ed. Orlando, FL: Harcourt, Brace Jovanovich.

Galbraith, M. W. 1991. The adult learning transactional process. In *Facilitating adult learning: A transactional process*, ed. M. W. Galbraith, 1–32. Malabar, FL: Robert E. Krieger.

Galbraith, M. W., and Zelenak, B. S. 1991. Adult learning methods and techniques. In *Facilitating adult learning: A transactional process*, ed. M. W. Galbraith, 103–33. Malabar, FL: Robert E. Krieger.

Garrison, R. 1987. The role of technology in continuing education. In *Continuing education in the year 2000*, ed. R. G.

Brockett, 41–53. New Directions for Continuing Education, no. 36. San Francisco: Jossey-Bass.

Gilligan, C. 1982. *In a different voice: Psychological theory and women's development*. Cambridge, MA: Harvard University Press.

Guglielmino, L. M., and Guglielmino, P. J. 1988. Self-directed learning in business and industry: An information age imperative. In *Self-directed learning: Application & theory*, ed. H. B. Long and Associates, 125–48. Athens, GA: Department of Adult Education, The University of Georgia.

Harris, L. 1988. Presidential views of social accountability in continuing education. *Canadian Journal of University Continuing Education*, 14(1): 3–10.

Hartree, A. 1984. Malcolm Knowles' theory of andragogy: A critique. *International Journal of Lifelong Learning*, 3(3): 203–10.

Havighurst, R. J. 1972. *Developmental tasks and education*. 3d ed. New York: McKay.

Hayes, E., ed. 1989. *Effective teaching styles*. New Directions for Continuing Education, no. 43. San Francisco: Jossey-Bass.

Hergenhahn, B. R. 1988. *An introduction to theories of learning*. 3d ed. Englewood Cliffs, NJ: Prentice-Hall.

Hiemstra, R. 1988. Translating personal values and philosophy into practical action. In *Ethical issues in adult education*, ed. R. G. Brockett, 178–94. New York: Teachers College Press.

Hodgetts, R. M. 1987. *Effective supervision: A practical approach*. New York: McGraw-Hill.

Holmberg-Wright, K. 1982. The budget as a planning instrument. In *Creative financing and budgeting*, ed. T. Shipp, 23–40. New Directions for Continuing Education, no. 16. San Francisco: Jossey-Bass.

Holt, M. E., and Lopos, G. L., eds. 1991. *Perspectives on educational certificate programs*. New Directions for Adult and Continuing Education, no. 52. San Francisco: Jossey-Bass.

Houle, C. O. 1956. Professional education for educators of adults. *Adult Education*, 6(3): 131–41.

———. 1961. *The inquiring mind.* Madison, WI: University of Wisconsin Press.

Illich, I. 1970. *Deschooling society.* New York: Harper & Row.

Jarvis, P. 1985. *The sociology of adult and continuing education.* London: Croom Helm.

———. 1987. *Adult learning in the social context.* London: Croom Helm.

Johnstone, J., and Rivera, R. J. 1965. *Volunteers for learning: A study of the educational pursuits of American adults.* Chicago: Aldine.

Jones, R. K. 1984. *Sociology of adult education.* Brookfield, VT: Gower.

Kidd, J. R. 1950. *Adult education in Canada.* Toronto: Canadian Association for Adult Education.

———. 1973. *How adults learn.* New York: Cambridge.

King, B. K., and Lerner, A. W. 1987. Organizational structure and performance dynamics in continuing education administration. *Continuing Higher Education Review,* 51(3): 21–38.

Knowles, M. S. 1975. *Self-directed learning: A guide for learners and teachers.* New York: Cambridge.

———. 1977. *A history of the adult education movement in the United States.* Revised and updated. New York: Cambridge.

Knowles, M. S. 1980. *The modern practice of adult education: From pedagogy to andragogy* (2d ed.). New York: Cambridge.

Knox, A. B., ed. 1979. *Assessing the impact of continuing education.* New Directions for Continuing Education, no. 3. San Francisco: Jossey-Bass.

———. 1986. *Helping adults learn.* San Francisco: Jossey-Bass.

Kolb, D. A. 1981. Learning styles and disciplinary differences. In *The modern American college,* ed. A. W. Chickering and Associates, 232–55. San Francisco: Jossey-Bass.

Kops, W. J., and Percival, A. 1990. The focus group interview: A research technique for program planners. *Canadian Journal of University Continuing Education*, 12: 31–38.

Kotler, P. 1985. *Marketing management: Analysis, planning and control* . 5th ed. Englewood Cliffs, NJ: Prentice-Hall.

Kotler, P., and Fox, K. 1985. *Strategic marketing for educational institutions.* Englewood Cliffs, NJ: Prentice-Hall.

Kowalski, T. J. 1988. *The organization and planning of adult education.* Albany, NY: State University of New York Press.

Kulich, J. 1991. Current trends and priorities in Canadian adult education. *International Journal of Lifelong Education*, 10(2): 93–106.

Lawson, K. H. 1975. Philosophical concepts and values in adult education. Nottingham, England: Barnes and Humby, Ltd.

Leffel, L. G. 1983. *Designing brochures for results.* Manhattan, KS: Learning Resources Network (LERN).

Levinson, D. J. 1986. A conception of adult development. *American Psychologist*, 41(1): 3–13.

Lewis, C. H., and Dunlop, C. C. 1991. Successful and unsuccessful adult education programs: Perceptions, explanations, and implications. In *Mistakes made and lessons learned: Overcoming obstacles to successful program planning,* ed. T. J. Sork. New Directions for Adult and Continuing Education, no. 49. San Francisco: Jossey-Bass.

Lewis, L. 1989. New educational technologies for the future. In *Handbook of adult and continuing education,* ed. S. B. Merriam and P. M. Cunningham, 613–27. San Francisco: Jossey-Bass.

Lindeman, E. C. 1989. *The meaning of adult education.* Norman, OK: Oklahoma Research Center for Continuing and Professional Education. (Original work published in 1926.)

Long, H. B. 1990. Understanding adult learners. In *Adult learning methods: A guide for effective instruction,* ed. M. W. Galbraith, 23–38. Malabar, FL: Robert E. Krieger.

Lotz, J., and Welton, M. R. 1987. "Knowledge for the people":

The origins and development of the Antigonish Movement. In *Knowledge for the people: The struggle for adult learning in English-speaking Canada, 1828–1973,* ed. M. R. Welton, 97–111. Toronto: OISE Press.

Lovett, T.; Clarke, C.; and Kilmurray, A. 1983. *Adult education and community action: Adult education and popular social movements.* London: Croom Helm.

Lund, B., and McGechaen, S. 1981. *CE programmer's manual.* Victoria, BC: Ministry of Education.

Lussier, R. N. 1989. *Supervision: A skill-building approach.* Homewood, IL: Irwin.

Lynton, E. A., and Elman, S. E. 1987. *New priorities for the university.* San Francisco: Jossey-Bass.

McKenzie, L. 1988. Philosophical orientations of adult educators (1985). In *Training educators of adults: The theory and practice of graduate adult education,* ed. S. D. Brookfield, 211–16. New York: Routledge.

Mager, R. F. 1984. *Developing attitude toward learning or SMATs'n'SMUTs.* 2d ed. Belmont, CA: Lake.

Maslow, A. H. 1970. *Motivation and personality.* 2d ed. New York: Harper & Row.

Merriam, S. B., ed. 1982. *Linking philosophy and practice.* New Directions for Continuing Education, no. 15. San Francisco: Jossey-Bass.

———. 1984. *Selected writings on philosophy and adult education.* Malabar, FL: Robert E. Krieger, 1984.

Merriam, S. B. 1988. Training adult educators in North America (1985). In *Training educators of adults: The theory and practice of graduate adult education,* ed. S. D. Brookfield, 30–40. New York: Routledge.

Merriam, S. B., and Caffarella, R. S. 1991. *Learning in adulthood.* San Francisco: Jossey-Bass.

Mezirow, J. 1984a. Review of principles of good practice in continuing education. *Lifelong Learning* 8(3): 27–28.

————. 1984b. A critical theory of adult learning and education. In *Selected writings on philosophy and adult education*, ed. S. B. Merriam, 123–39. Malabar, FL: Robert E. Krieger.

————. 1991. *Transformative dimensions of adult learning*. San Francisco: Jossey-Bass.

Miller, J. V., and Musgrove, M. L., eds. 1986. *Issues in adult career counselling*. New Directions for Continuing Education, no. 32. San Francisco: Jossey-Bass.

Monette, M. L. 1979. Needs assessment: A critique of philosophical assumptions. *Adult Education*, 29(2): 85–95.

Murk, P. J., and Galbraith, M. W. 1986. Planning successful continuing education programs: A systems approach model. *Lifelong Learning*, 9(5): 21–23.

Nadler, L. 1982. *Designing training programs*. Reading: Addison-Wesley.

Nilson, C. 1989. *Training program workbook and kit*. Englewood Cliffs, NJ: Prentice-Hall.

Paterson, R. W. K. 1979. Values, education and the adult. Boston: Routledge and Kegan Paul.

Patton, M. Q. 1990. *Qualitative evaluation and research methods*. 2d ed. Newbury Park, CA: Sage.

Peters, J. M. 1991. Strategies for reflective practice. In *Professional development for educators of adults*, ed. R. G. Brockett, 89–96. New Directions for Adult and Continuing Education, no. 51. San Francisco: Jossey-Bass.

Pratt, D. D. 1988. Andragogy as a relational construct. *Adult Education Quarterly*, 38(3): 160–81.

Quigley, B. A., ed. 1989. *Fulfilling the promise of adult and continuing education*. New Directions for Continuing Education, no. 44. San Francisco: Jossey-Bass.

————. 1990. Hidden logic: Reproduction and resistance in adult literacy and adult basic education. *Adult Education Quarterly*, 40(2): 103–15.

Rados, D. L. 1981. *Marketing for nonprofit organizations*. Boston: Arbour House.

Renner, P. F. 1983. *The instructor's survival kit: A handbook for teachers of adults.* 2d ed. Vancouver: Training Associates Ltd.

Roberts, H. 1985. Peace education and university continuing education. *Canadian Journal of University Continuing Education,* 11(2): 86–93.

Rogers, C. R. 1969. *Freedom to learn.* Westerville, OH: Merrill.

Rogoff, R. L. 1987. *The training wheel: A simple model for instructional design.* New York: Wiley.

Ross-Gordon, J. M.; Martin, L. G.; and Buck Briscoe, D. 1990. *Serving culturally diverse populations.* New Directions for Adult and Continuing Education, no. 48. San Francisco: Jossey-Bass.

Rossman, M. H., and Bunning, R. L. 1988. Knowledge and skills for the adult educator: A delphi study (1978). In *Training educators of adults: The theory and practice of graduate adult education,* ed. S. D. Brookfield, 150–67. New York: Routledge.

Scanlan, C. S., and Darkenwald, G. G. 1984. Identifying deterrents to participation in continuing education. *Adult Education Quarterly,* 34(3): 155–66.

Schindler-Rainman, E., and Lippit, R. 1975. *Taking your meetings out of the doldrums.* San Diego: University Associates.

Schlossberg, N.; Lynch, A.; and Chickering, A. 1989. *Improving higher education environments for adults.* San Francisco: Jossey-Bass.

Schön, D. A. 1983. *The reflective practitioner: How professionals think in action.* New York: Basic Books.

———. 1987. *Educating the reflective practitioner: Toward a new design for teaching and learning in the professions.* San Francisco: Jossey-Bass.

Schroeder, W. L. 1970. Adult education defined and described. In *Handbook of adult education,* ed. R. M. Smith; G. F. Aker; and J. R. Kidd. New York: Macmillan.

Selman, G. 1985. The adult educator: Change agent or program technician. *Canadian Journal of University Continuing Education,* 11: 77–86.

———. 1987. Adult education and citizenship, In *Choosing our future: Adult education and public policy in Canada,* ed. F. Cassidy and R. Farris, 36–49. Toronto: OISE Press.

Selman, G., and Dampier, P. 1991. *The foundations of adult education in Canada.* Toronto: Thompson.

Shipp, T., ed. 1982. *Creative financing and budgeting.* New Directions for Continuing Education, no. 16. San Francisco: Jossey-Bass.

Simerly, R. G., ed. 1987. *Strategic planning and leadership in continuing education.* San Francisco: Jossey-Bass.

Simerly, R. G. 1990. *Planning and marketing conferences and workshops.* San Francisco: Jossey-Bass.

Simerly, R. G., and Associates. 1989. *Handbook of marketing for continuing education.* San Francisco: Jossey-Bass.

Simpson, E. L. 1987. An interactive model of program development. In *Materials and methods in adult and continuing education,* ed. C. Klevens, 154–60. Los Angeles: Klevens.

Skinner, B. F. 1974. *About behaviorism.* New York: Knopf.

Smith, D. H., and Offerman, M. J. 1989. The management of adult and continuing education. In *Handbook of adult and continuing education,* ed. S. B. Merriam and P. M. Cunningham, 246–59. San Francisco: Jossey-Bass.

Smith, R. M. 1982. *Learning how to learn: Applied theory for adults.* New York: Cambridge.

Sork, T. J., ed. 1991. *Mistakes made and lessons learned: Overcoming obstacles to successful program planning.* New Directions for adult and continuing education, no. 49. San Francisco: Jossey-Bass.

Sork, T. J., and Caffarella, R. S. 1989. Planning programs for adults. In *Handbook of adult and continuing education,* ed. S. B. Merriam and P. M. Cunningham, 233–45. San Francisco: Jossey-Bass.

Spencer, B., and McIlroy, J. 1991. British university adult education in context: Lessons for Canada? *Canadian Journal of University Continuing Education,* 17(2): 21–40.

BIBLIOGRAPHY

Stabler, M. 1972. *Explorations in a night culture or after dinner walks in night school.* Toronto: Ontario Association for Continuing Education.

Steele, S. M. 1989. The evaluation of adult and continuing education. In *Handbook of adult and continuing education,* ed. S. B. Merriam and P. M. Cunningham, 260–72. San Francisco: Jossey-Bass.

Sternberg, R. J. 1985. *Beyond I.Q.: A triarchic theory of human intelligence.* Cambridge: Cambridge University Press.

———. 1990. Understanding adult intelligence. In *Intelligence and adult learning,* ed. R. A. Fellenz and G. J. Conti. Bozeman, MT: Center for Adult Learning.

Stubblefield, H. W. 1991. Making the most of professional reading. In *Professional development for educators of adults,* ed. R. B. Brockett, 25–34. New Directions for Adult and Continuing Education, no. 51. San Francisco: Jossey-Bass.

Tennant, M. 1988. *Psychology and adult learning.* London: Routledge.

Thompson, G. 1986. I'll know it when I see it: What is distance education? *Canadian Journal of University Continuing Education,* 12: 83–91.

Tough, A. 1971. *The adult's learning projects: A fresh approach to theory and practice in adult learning.* Toronto: Ontario Institute for Studies in Education.

———. 1978. Major learning efforts: Recent research and future directions. *Adult Education,* 28: 250–63.

———. 1979. *The adult's learning projects.* 2d ed. Toronto: Ontario Institute for Studies in Education.

Tyler, R. 1949. *Basic principles of curriculum and instruction.* Chicago: The University of Chicago Press.

UNESCO. 1980. *Recommendation on the development of adult education.* Ottawa: Canadian Commission for UNESCO.

Verner, C., and Booth, A. 1964. *Adult education.* Washington, DC: The Center for Applied Research in Education.

Waalen, J., and Wilson, L. 1991. *Policies and practices in certificate and diploma education in Canadian universities: Final report.* Toronto: Ryerson Polytechnic Institute.

Welton, M. R. 1987a. "On the eve of a great mass movement": Reflections on the origins of the CAAE. In *Choosing our future: Adult education and public policy in Canada,* ed. F. Cassidy and R. Farris, 12–35. Toronto: OISE Press.

Welton, M. R., ed. 1987b. *Knowledge for the people: The struggle for adult learning in English-speaking Canada, 1828–1973.* Toronto: OISE Press.

Whale, W. B. 1987. Leadership in the information society. *Canadian Journal of University Continuing Education,* 13(1): 75–81.

Wickett, R. E. Y.; Collins, M.; McKay, W. D.; and Plumb, D. 1987. *Adult education studies in Canada.* Saskatoon: University of Saskatchewan.

Wlodkowski, R. J. 1985. *Enhancing adult motivation to learn.* San Francisco: Jossey-Bass.

————. 1990. Strategies to enhance adult motivation to learn. In *Adult learning methods: A guide for effective instruction,* ed. M. W. Galbraith, 97–118. Malabar, FL: Robert E. Krieger.

Woolfe, R. S.; Murgatroyd, S.; and Rhys, S. 1987. *Guidance and counseling in adult and continuing education.* Milton Keyes: Open University Press.

Zinn, L. M. 1990. Identifying your philosophical orientation. In *Adult learning methods: A guide for effevtive instruction,* ed. M. W. Galbraith, 39–77. Malabar, FL: Robert E. Krieger.

Index

About the Author

Anne Percival, M.A., M.B.A., Ed.D., is currently the Associate Dean (Administration), Continuing Education Division, The University of Manitoba. She has over ten years' experience in continuing professional education, specializing in management development. Anne teaches courses in management and adult education, and her current research interests relate to barriers to participation in adult education. Anne has recently completed the Adult Education Guided Independent Study (AEGIS) Doctoral Program at Teachers College, Columbia University.